Robert Robertson

interwoven lines

TO CLAUDETTE

Thank you so much for all your help and support.

–
4

My books in the *scattering texts* series are counterpoints of texts and images which aim to open the subconscious channels of thought, memory, perception and emotion.

These are unique to each individual reader, so they can interact and mix unpredictably, without limits.

1. in the countries of the mind (2018)
2. intervals of clouds and sun (2019)
3. vertical gliding (2020)
4. a summer in Haiti (2023)
5. glances in winter (2023)
6. focus/distraction (2024)
7. reflections reflected (2024)
8. interwoven lines (2024)

- *Oserake and The River That Walks*

- *Machines* (start) from *Diversions*.

- *River* from *Diversions*, Al Frybas.

- *Encounter on Windy Island* and *The University of Wind* from *Rabelaisdada*.

- *MoneyBrandPoem* from *Rabelaisdada*.

- *Psychic Neon* from *Invisible City*.

- *East Side Morning* from *Invisible City*.

- *Empedocles*, Act 1 Scene 1.

   This will lead to five other scenes from my dance opera.

   The artist and filmmaker Dennis Dracup made the film for the music/film version of *Empedocles*.

Attributions are given at the back of this book,
under Origins

The texts and images in this book are
more or less randomly interwoven,
to stimulate a wide variety of
unexpected connections and
combinations.

biographical

Robertson has taught at the University of Kent (UK), The Netherlands Academy of Film and Television, the British Film Institute, and King's College London.

He worked for fourteen years at the American publisher Gordon and Breach and Harwood's London office, setting up an international music, theatre and dance publishing programme.

His music/films have been shown at the universities of Oxford, Cambridge, McGill, Nice-Sophia Antipolis, Canterbury Christchurch, University College London, amongst others, and at various venues, including the Whitechapel Gallery, the ICA, the Hundred Years Gallery (London), MUDAM Luxembourg, the Béla Balàsz Foundation (Budapest), The Linhart Foundation (Prague), Synchronicity Space (New York).

websites

1. ocatillo audiovisual

2. Robert Robertson, British Music Collection

3. Robert Robertson amazon.co.uk (for books)

It's chance which reveals existence to us from day to day.

Georges Braque.

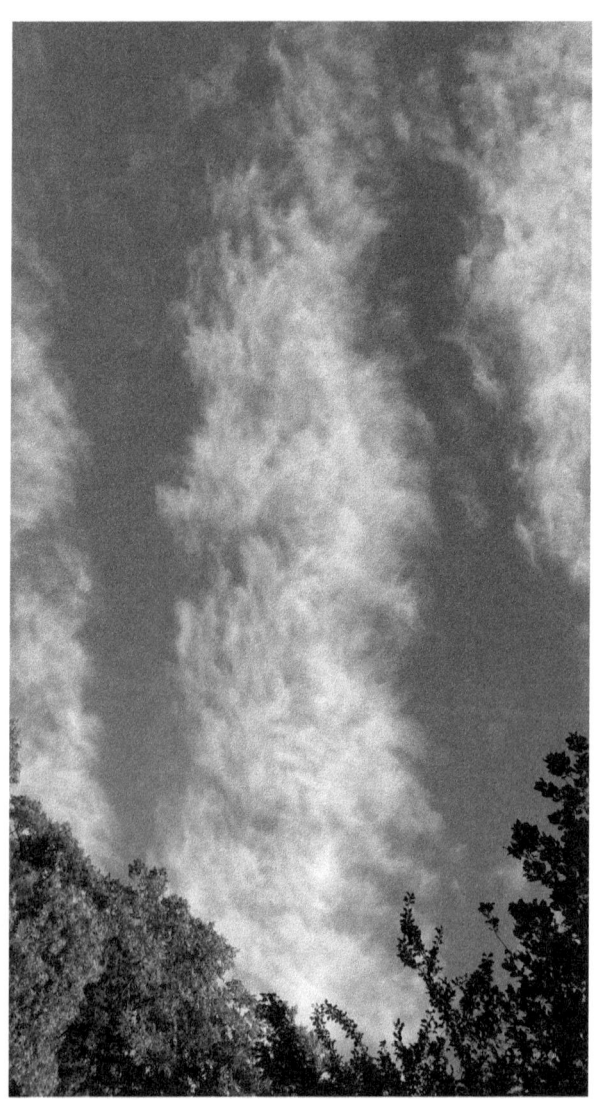

1. verticals

2. multi-dimensional inspiration

Cartier-Bresson believes that like
poetry or music, photography is a
means of expression - the important
thing is to be sensitive.

He emphasizes that
'you must nourish
your mind constantly
with music, art,
painting'.

He mentions his passion
for J.S. Bach and Mozart,
and their clarity of expression.

Also, his enthusiasm for an extensive
choice of painters:
Paolo Uccello,
Piero della Francesca,
Titian,
Jan van Eyck,
Goya,
Daumier,
Seurat,
Cézanne,
Degas,
Bonnard, and the mysterious
Las Meninas by Velázquez.

And Cartier-Bresson also mentions
the writers who have influenced him:

Montaigne,
Saint-Simon,
Elisée Reclus,
Stendhal,
Flaubert,
Lautréamont,
Bakunin,
Proust,
Joyce,

and the poets
Baudelaire,
and Rimbaud.

He mentions that
Proust and Saint-Simon have a
strong visual sense -

photographers should read them.

And also
Parmenides,
Heraclitus,
Lao-tzu,
the Buddha,
and Nietzsche.

These philosophers inspire him.

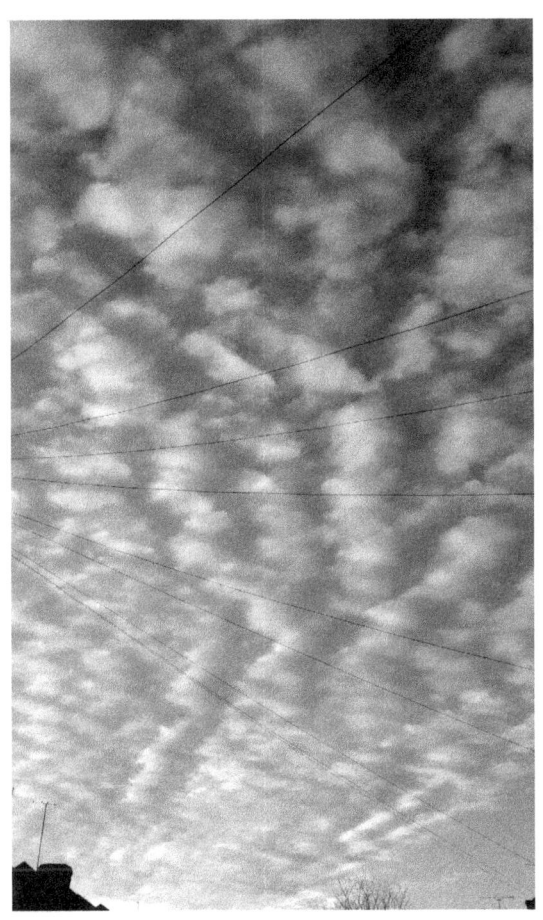

3. radiating

4. memories

Memories have echoes, just like sounds

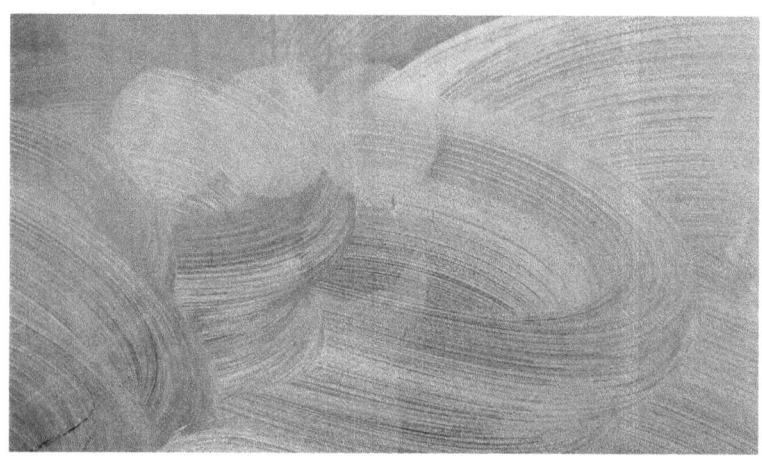

5. whirlings

6. categories

I've always liked Leonard Bernstein, as he
didn't limit himself to pre-existing categories.
And I feel that one of the great things about
James Joyce's *Ulysses* is that it contains
so much, that it effectively defies the limits
of previous categories.

One of the themes in my current *scattering texts*
series is this question of categories - thinking
about it, it's related to the idea of sets, developed
by the mathematician Georg Cantor.

7. tangibility

Of the very few things I could grasp in my maths lessons at school, one of them was set theory, as it was presented as being related to recognisable objects, as opposed to the usual routine of being introduced to purely abstract principles, with no indication of any link to tangible things.

How set theory brought about Russell's Paradox also intrigued me.

Recently I've realised that the problems my work poses for those with an academic turn of mind is due to its leaping over the limits of categories. The concept of the academic job is itself based on the dominance of categories - and so inevitably it attracts this approach: entire working lives can be spent fitting things into neat categories, and devising new categories in order to do so, *ad nauseam*.

This is why I admire the Bauhaus teachers so much - they broke open categories, and they were *practitioners* too.

I do think that the work of artists is inevitably related to their personal experiences in some form or another, so that part of it is autobiographical - but the latter category does have open borders, and it's this permeable quality that is one of the things I find exciting about art in its variety of forms - like science too, when scientists look beyond the borders that have been imposed on them.

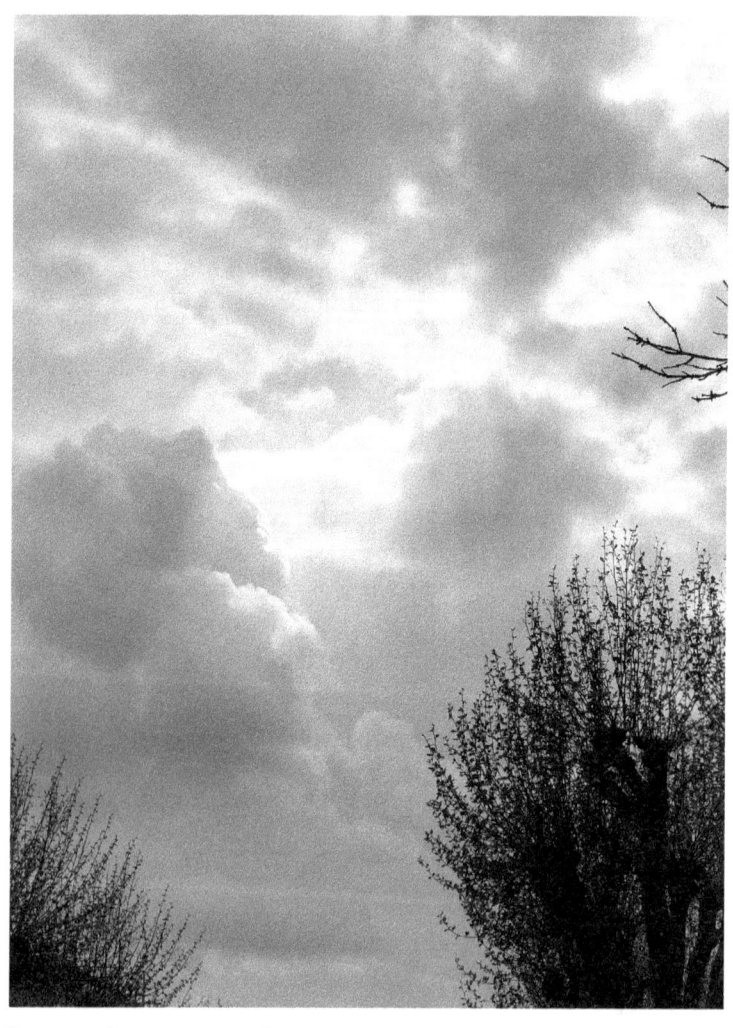

8. complex perspectives

9. precision, inspiration

If he had to choose between his scientific work or his literary work, which one would he choose?
'It would be unthinkable,' he replies, 'to have to choose just one of them, as they elevate each other: the precision of poetry and the inspiration of science'.
Here Nabokov reverses what might have been a cliché: 'the inspiration of poetry and the precision of science.'
In this way he interweaves his two approaches to life.

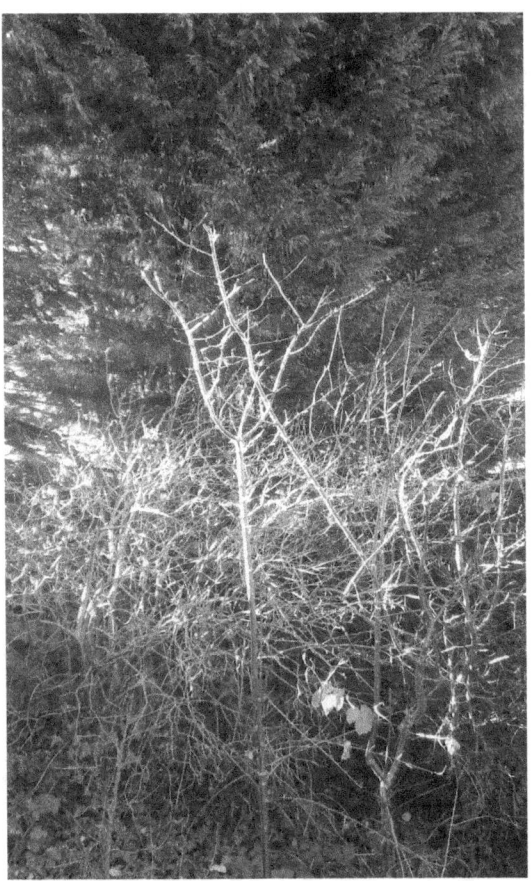

10. early spring dance

11. the bigger picture

Artists who have real talent don't complain that they've been misunderstood by their contemporaries - on the contrary, they actually draw from this incomprehension a certainty of their survival
in the future.

12. inexplicable

In art there is only one thing that matters:
what cannot be explained.

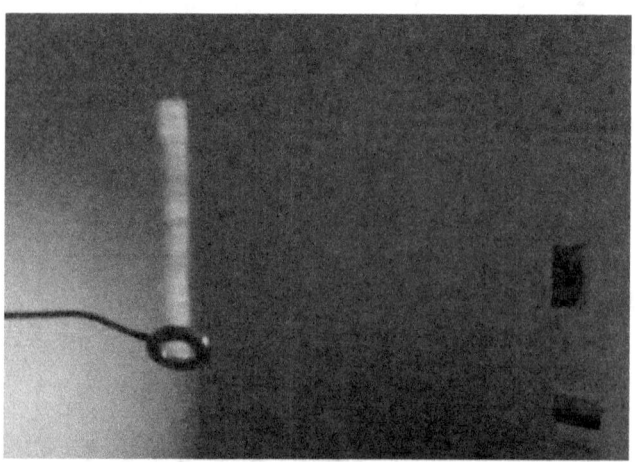

13. a chance encounter

14. categorical

It's all very well, but you can't call *that* a symphony.

William Walton's above comment on Mahler's *Third Symphony*, is surprising, given that he said this fifty years after this symphony's hugely successful première in Krefeld in 1904. Despite challenging rehearsal circumstances, due to an orchestra being assembled at the last minute, Mahler received a standing ovation for this work, and favourable reviews from the local critics.

Walton's dismissal of Mahler's *Third Symphony* is all the more surprising, as on a few occasions Walton's own work, across his output, occasionally did break with pre-existing musical categories. An example is *Façade*, in which his music was combined with Edith Sitwell reading her poetry - it was first performed in 1923.

And his colourful and rhythmically energetic cantata *Belshazzar's Feast* (1931), features selections from the bible chosen by Osbert Sitwell. These texts are sung and enunciated in various ways by the two choirs, in a score that also features an orchestra and two brass bands, and a part for solo baritone.

These two works by Walton provide a foretaste of Luciano Berio's diverse use of the spoken voice over his remarkable collage of music by different composers (including himself) in his *Sinfonia* (1968/69).

In this very lively work there's a collage of quotes from Mayakovsky, Beckett, Joyce, Lévi-Strauss and others, that are spoken, sung, whispered and shouted by a group of eight voices.

And lastly, there's Walton's music for the climactic aerial battle at the end of the film *The Battle of Britain* (1969), directed by Guy Hamilton, for which the roar of the airplanes' engines, the rattling of their guns, and the noise when they explode, are cut out, and there's just Walton's music, and initially, the voices of the pilots.

The result is extraordinarily exciting, but it's also deeply disturbing, as we witness a pilot failing to eject as flames rapidly reach him, and we see others losing control of their aircraft, as they plunge, crashing on the beach, or into the sea.

The overall effect of this memorable sequence is of the horrors of aerial battle, in contrast with the curves of the soaring and diving of the aircraft, choreographed in a powerful but surprisingly elegant audiovisual counterpoint: Walton's music, in total contrast with the sporadic visual nightmares.

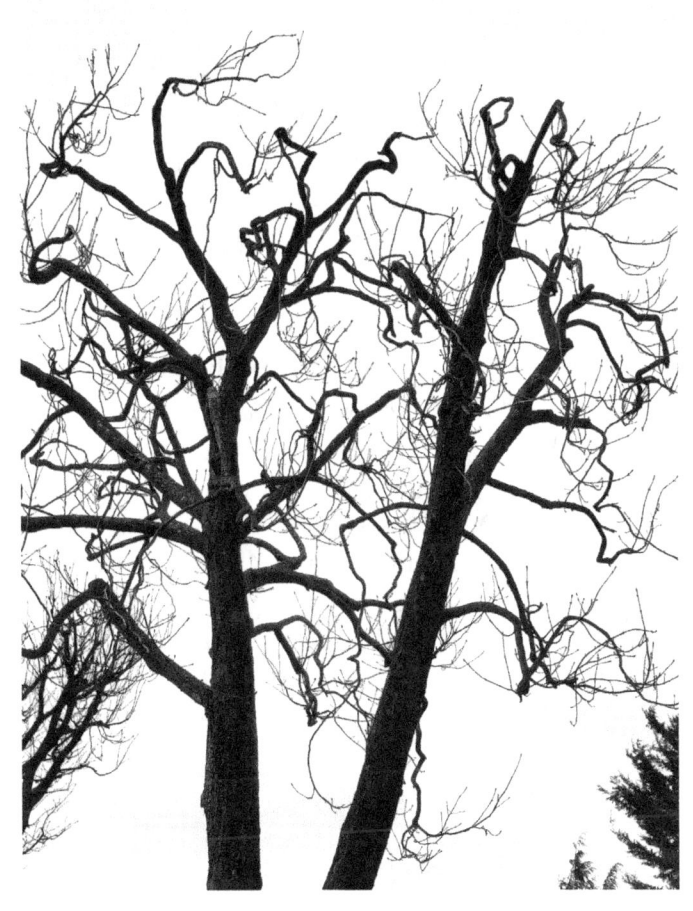

15. trees in winter, dancing

16. composition by fragments

When asked about how he starts a novel,
whether it's with a character or a story,
he replies that he begins with neither of
these things - what stimulates his writing
are 'colours, pictures, visions'.

This is why he doesn't begin at the beginning,
or end at the end - and he never proceeds
chronologically.

Instead he starts anywhere, then shifts to
somewhere else to write a very different image,
then he fills in the holes between these fragments.

Nabokov's description of his writing process
resembles what he does when butterfly-hunting.

17. danger

Go straight into the heart of danger,
for there you will find safety.

(Presumably this means that you should
find out as much as you can about the
nature of the danger, and that way
neutralise it).

18. struggles

My work for an American academic
publisher (14 years),
and my experiences as a student at
various universities (12 years), gave me
the opportunity to meet academics
across the world, in a wide variety of
institutions and disciplines.

And nowhere did I find anyone who
wasn't engaged in some form of
Machiavellian struggle for their existence!

And I'll never forget (as a key part of my job),
meeting my first academic - there he was,
tall (even when seated) waiting for a
music lecture to start, at a university
somewhere in the middle of the United
States, as he looked down at me from above,
silently, whenever I said anything.

Of course I didn't bother following up
this 'meeting'.

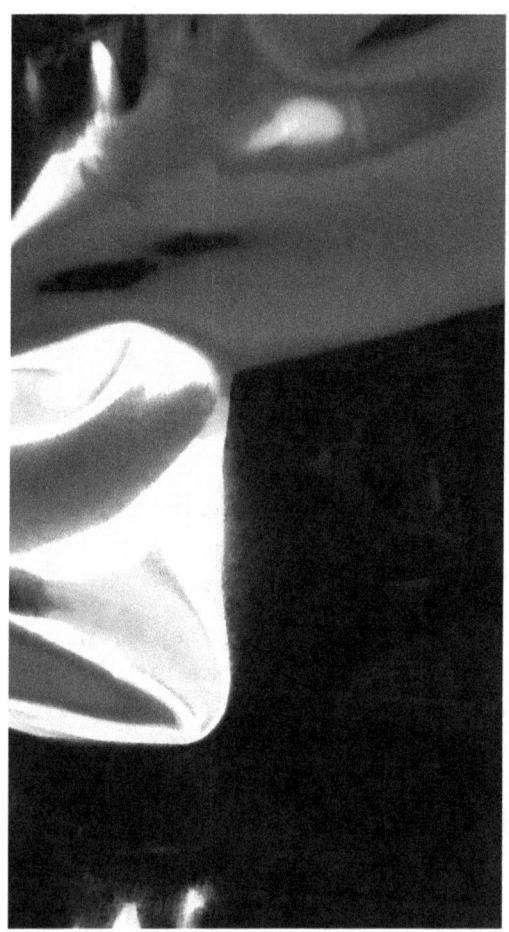

19. birdhead

20. openings

Closed doors open the realisation of new forms,
beyond the imaginings of the closers of doors.

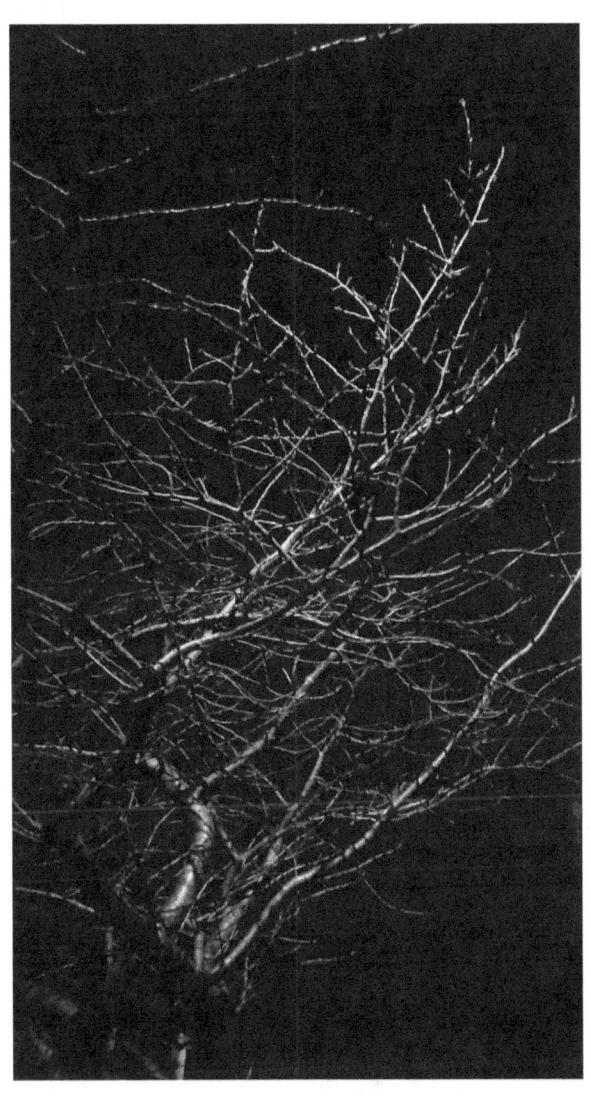

21. nocturnal energy

22. communicating photographs

When photographs are published in a book,
it's as if they become a kind of permanent exhibition.

23. jobs-for-life

One of the much-prized advantages of the academic
career is perceived to be the 'job-for-life'.

The disadvantage here is that fractious academic politics
can make this supposed benefit more like a life sentence.

But why is this surprising?

After all, one needs to look at the origins of this type
of 'job-for-life': they point to the monasteries from which
universities developed, and which had necessarily more to
do with belief than with ability.

You began as a nun or monk, and you mostly ended as a
nun or monk.

You might even have risen through the monastic ranks,
but you remained in the same basic institution - for life.

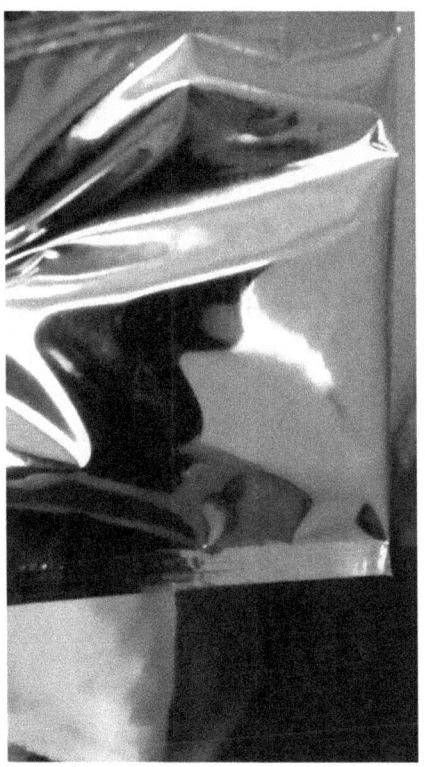

24. waiting to pounce

25. unreal

The real unreality is the conventional and the common.

26. limited

Academic jargon can be a form of mental prison.

27. a symmetry of pipes

Long ago, in the course of my publishing work I'd occasionally find myself meeting those who appeared to be 'gatekeepers' - fortunately rarely, and usually mostly easily forgotten.

They shared a bi-laterally symmetrical characteristic, as they tended to reflect the opinions of others.

Often slightly sarcastic, they'd have no problems with things as they were, as their function depended on those in authority in a particular domain.

However, I do recall one, as on his desk he had a rack of eight pipes.

For me that was the most interesting bi-laterally symmetrical thing about this encounter.

The meeting fortunately didn't last long, as none of these symmetrically arranged pipes were smoked.

28. humour

Humour is really a loss of balance - and an appreciation of losing it…it involves a fast and free association of values.

29. scattering texts

Where did the bookshop put my *scattering texts* ?

At first they were in the Essays section.

Then they migrated to the Poetry section.

Now they're in the Fiction section.

But *scattering texts* aren't fiction.

It's like displaying *Alice in Wonderland*

in the Politics and Current Affairs section.

Except that it's the other way round:

'fiction' in 'facts' (Lewis Carroll),

as opposed to 'facts' in 'fiction':

scattering texts.

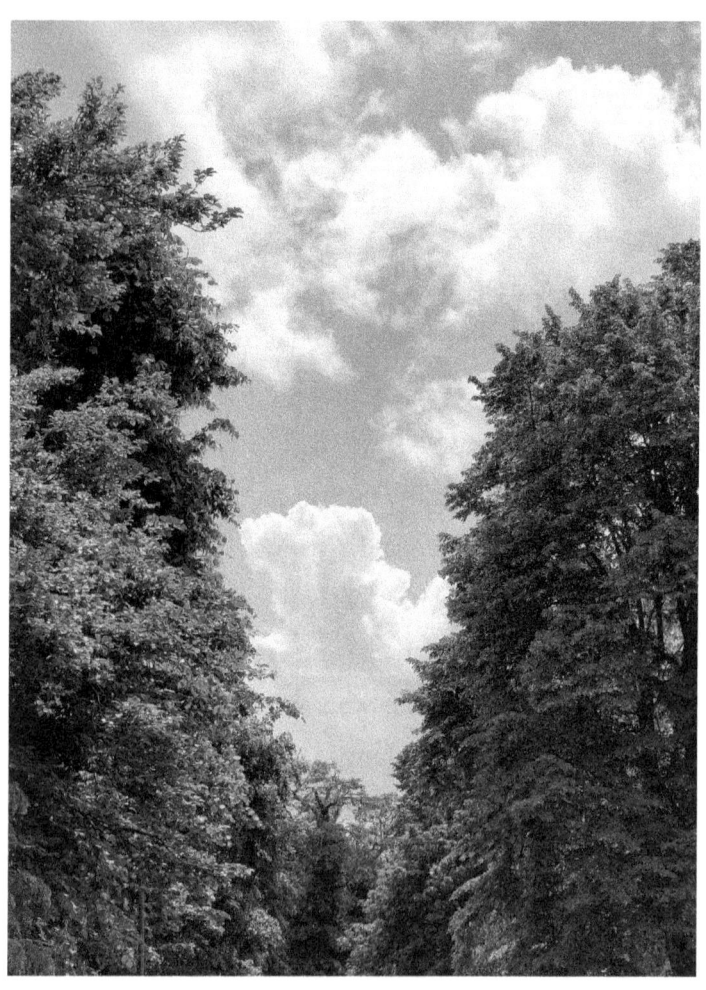

30. multiple spaces

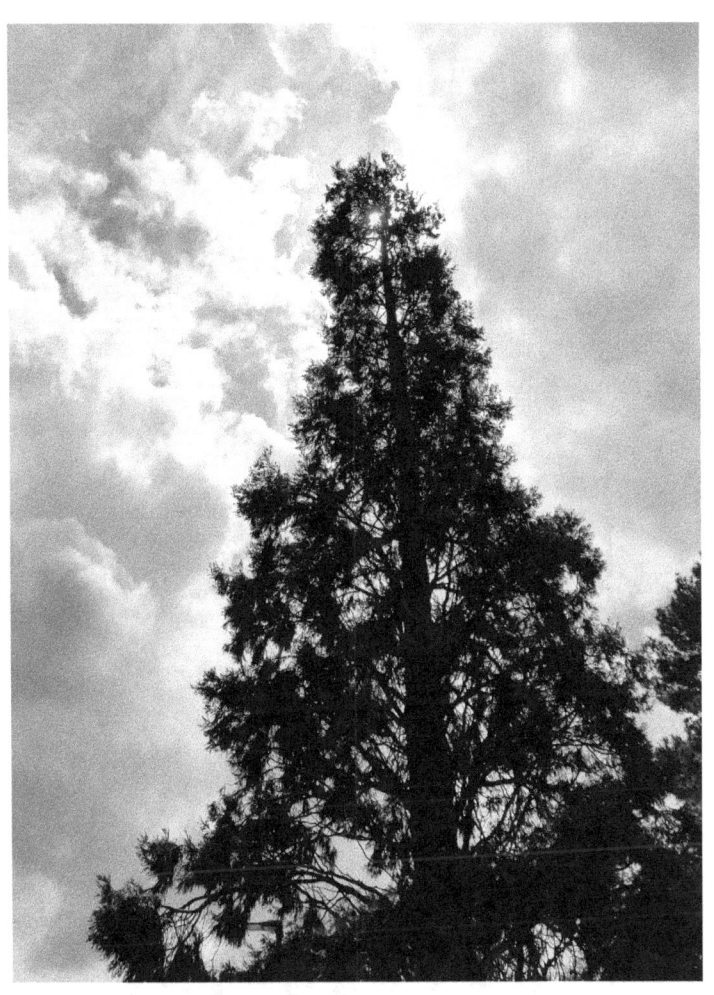

31. soaring

32. choice from chaos

You have to choose from what surrounds you, so that in your work, you can balance the meaning and form that you're deriving from this chaotic flood of reality.

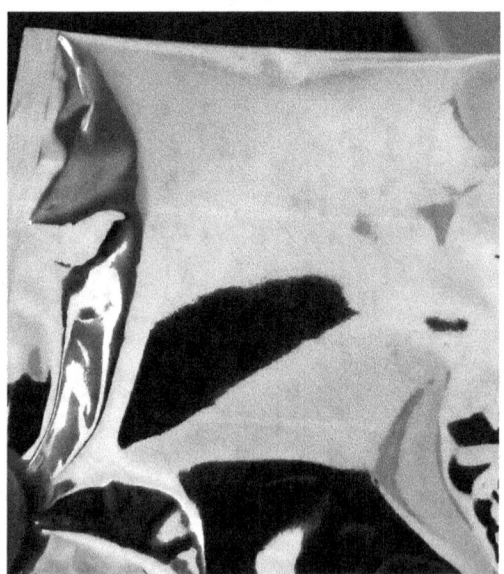

33. foxy

34. authority figure

I cannot recall anything memorable
being said at a meeting with an
authority figure.

Why?

These meetings were dominated (I can't
remember the exact details) by general
concerns to do with developments
regarding possible territorial incursions,
their territory being the dominant subject.
Fear is a key ingredient here, accompanied
by a strong lack of openness, resulting in
rather narrow points of view.

This territorial behaviour brings to my mind
military images - especially the symmetry of
uniforms, at the centre of which lies power,
which attempts to exert itself identically on
all possible fronts.

This approach also breeds a dull form of
repetition: predictable, like marching in step,
a mental uniformity - resulting in a totally
symmetrical form of thought.

On one occasion I found myself at a meeting with someone, at a large round table.

From the start, I couldn't help noticing that the person I was meeting made sure that their place was directly opposite me: here the symmetrical thinking had immediately transferred itself into a dialectically confrontational bi-laterally symmetrical space.

And the result of this meeting?

A complete waste of time for both of us.

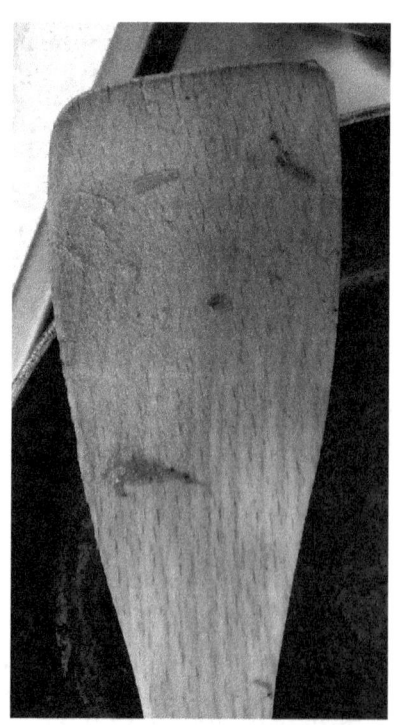

35. focussing on the essentials

36. generalisations

The phenomenon of generalisation is caused by what he calls a demon of generalisations - he tells us how this demon attaches little labels to everything it encounters.

37. unpredictable

Unpredictable rejections have always been a valuable source of creative ideas.

The usual career path after a good first degree, is to continue and obtain a good postgraduate degree.

This normal pathway also applies to composers, except that in my case, my approach didn't match the current fashionable aesthetic of the time.

So I taught music in schools, which happened to be a very exciting time for this subject: I gained experience in conducting choirs and orchestras.

And at my last music teaching post, the American musician Janice Rieman was the very dynamic and creative Head of the Music Department, in a school where we taught in a warehouse, so that with our students we could create and perform music as softly and as loudly as we wanted.

And in my classes I worked with a wide diversity of small ensembles - we were supplied with all kinds of instruments, of excellent quality.

We would experiment with combining music and words, various kinds of singing techniques, choral experiments, music theatre scenes, improvisations with all kinds of combinations of instruments, including those being learned by students who had instrumental teachers.

I even composed music for the school orchestra, which I rehearsed and conducted, in a creative environment where I learned as much as I taught.

Once, I looked after a class of around sixty students, as a teacher was absent that day.

As a result, there were too many to do group performances with instruments, so I divided this huge class into two choirs, and I conducted and recorded them in a choral improvisation, which involved continuously changing harmonies, and various interweaving glissandi.

Then I played them the recording of their performance and we listened in amazement to what they had just sung!

These experiments inspired the choral music I composed several years later, for several scenes in my dance opera, *Empedocles*.

And my teaching music in schools in central London introduced me to the exciting diversity of music and dance from the various traditions in the Caribbean islands, which inspired me to compose a new kind of opera, *The Kingdom*, a complete unity of music, dance, and theatre.

First I wrote the libretto for it, which I based on *The Kingdom of This World*, the Cuban writer Alejo Carpentier's novel about the Haitian Revolution.

Then I spent six weeks in Haiti, visiting the historical locations which feature in the work, as well as attending a variety of traditional *vaudou* ceremonies, and being inspired by their complete unity of music, dance and theatre.*

And I was very lucky to have a dynamic, well-rehearsed and sold-out production of my first opera at the Engelenbak Theatre in Amsterdam in 1984, directed by the American theatre director and choreographer Rufus Collins, and the Surinamese theatre director, Henk Tjon.

This was just before opera returned to its old traditional venues and performance practices - when it became something to which people would take their business clients, to impress them.

At this time I started to work for an American publishing company, where my job was to revive the beginnings of an international contemporary music publishing programme. I then set up international contemporary dance and theatre publishing lists.

All these activities led to my meeting establishment, as well as non-establishment people the world over: composers, musicologists, choreographers, dramatists, poets, and theatre directors.

I developed the publishing programme to include theatre, mime, and poetry in performance, thereby making possible the inclusion of innovative cross-fertilisations between music, dance, theatre and poetry, internationally, including publishing videotapes and music recordings.

I soon realized that had I been recommended for this publishing job by a UK music establishment figure, I would likely have had to limit my publishing programme to symmetrically reflect a narrow and officially supported taste and approach.

Fortunately I've been lucky with Americans, and later with a Canadian, the filmmaker Professor Marielle Nitoslawska, at the Mel Hoppenheim School of Cinema, in Montreal.

In her Film Production class she supported the making of my music/film portrait of Montreal in winter: *Oserake and The River That Walks*.

(As I'd not been able to find anyone in London's educational establishments who had the slightest interest in a composer who wanted to make music/films!).

---

* In *a summer in Haiti* (No 5 in my scattering texts book series) I provide an account of the most extraordinary experiences I had in Haiti, when I was doing vital research there for all aspects of my first opera, *The Kingdom*, in the summer of 1981.

38. creative legacy

I cannot be grasped in the here and now,
for I reside just as much with the dead
as with the unborn.
Somewhat closer to the heart of creation
than usual, but not nearly close enough.

39. the nature of poetry

Poetry includes two elements that are
suddenly in conflict - a spark between
two elements. It just comes by nurturing
yourself and living fully by submerging
yourself in reality.

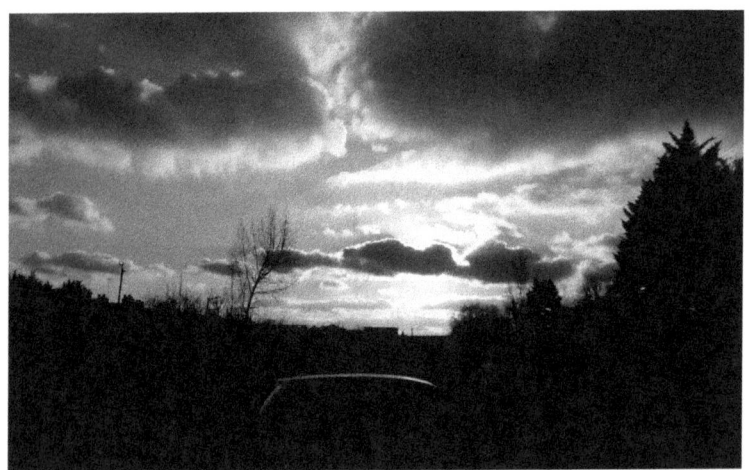

40. games of light

41. realities

Nabokov does not believe in the existence of what is
called an objective reality.
He affirms that the combinations invented by the artist
can give us a new form of reality, unique to the work.
For me, this approach to creativity is refreshingly
opposite to the social realist, 'kitchen sink' method,
in which a belief in the existence of an objective reality
is seen as being 'real'.

42. the disparaging club

Over the years I've had encounters, meetings, even lunches, with a member of the disparaging club.

The characteristics of the members of this club are straightforward: they don't dismiss what their colleagues are dismissing - in fact they look around and absorb the prevailing disparagements of the day, and repeat them to check if you are (or are not) a member of their disparaging club.

These meetings were the least memorable of all, and the disparagements were always offered with a knowing smile.

43. risk of merit

Of merit one demands modesty; but those who ostentatiously run down merit are listened to with relish.

44. ordering hierarchies

Why hierarchical classification?

An obsession with labels, boxes, cans,

in order of excellence - this is where

thinking stops and the academic

processing of information begins.

45. extreme academia

I once came across a book in which the academic author had listed all the times that J.S. Bach had re-cycled parts of his vast and extensively varied output.

But why didn't this academic author find a better use of his time?

It's a perfect example of working within a specific category, to the exclusion of everything else.

In fact this book deals with a category of a category of a category.

The logical conclusion of this kind of approach would ultimately end with a list of how many times (for example) J.S. Bach uses semiquavers (or even accidentals) in the multi-volume collection of his works:
a category of a category of a category of a category.

46. to be aware beyond style

To continually scan life - to notice something

that catches your eye in the continuous stream

that's around you all the time - this is something

that lies beyond style.

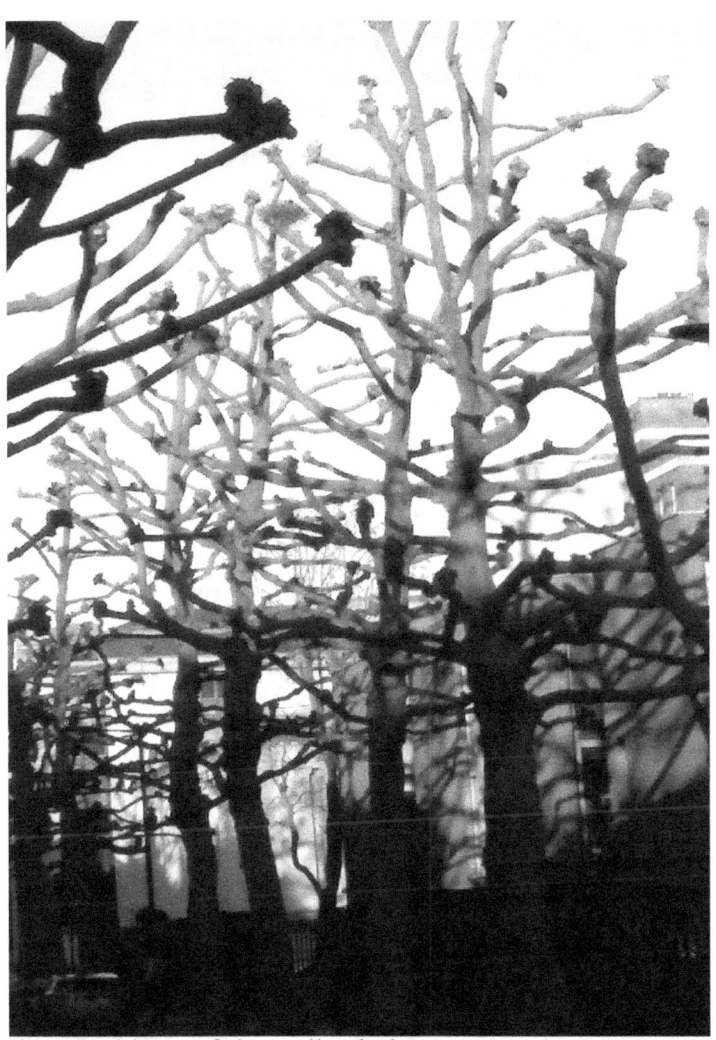

47. clashings of the pollarded

48. challenging cacti

'Cacti show a wide variety of growth habits,
which are difficult to divide into clear, simple
categories'.

I like the resilient quality in cacti, and I enjoyed the
astonishing varieties of them I saw on walks through
the Arizona desert, near Tucson. Some have
beguiling names, for example the alarming cactus
known as *Mother-in-Law's Cushion.*

49. truth in relation

Truth isn't absolute: it always has a relationship to
something, to a context.

And artists establish relationships, whether these
are expressed in photography, poetry, painting,
and also love.

This can be seen in Sergei Parajanov's
three-dimensional collages, in which he smashes
dishes, cuts up reproductions of paintings, and
incorporates a variety of objects, in order to
create new relationships between things, by
exploding them.

And Nabokov's very brief dreamlike audiovisual
memory sequence also comes to mind:
'in just one radiant moment a boy passes by
whistling a tune, a puddle reflects a branch, he
hears excited birds in an old garden in the rain,
as an old long-dead friend closes his dripping
umbrella, smiling.'

50. my first interview

My increasing inability to walk, due to a congenital malformation in both feet, required two six-hour operations, and a year of treatment.

For a ten-year-old, this was a long interruption in life, away from school. But fortunately, as a result, I was able to walk again.

My next challenge was an interview with a rather surly headmaster of a junior school.

(The results of the arithmetic test he'd given me had not impressed him).

He asked me what I was reading, and I told him about the *Observer Illustrated Pocketbook* which features drawings of different styles of architecture in Britain, from across the centuries.

I was finding this little book fascinating - I explained that it would enable me to look out for and identify these buildings' styles, to find out when they were built, and why they looked the way they did... after a year away from being able to walk, this seemed to me to be an attractive prospect.

The headmaster was appalled.

Perhaps he would have been happier if I'd been reading the *Observer Illustrated Pocketbook of British Medals and Awards* ?

This first experience of an interview was to be very useful for a whole host of interviews I was later to experience - some of them would also feature similarly seemingly unbridgeable gaps between the interests of the interviewer and the interviewee.

___

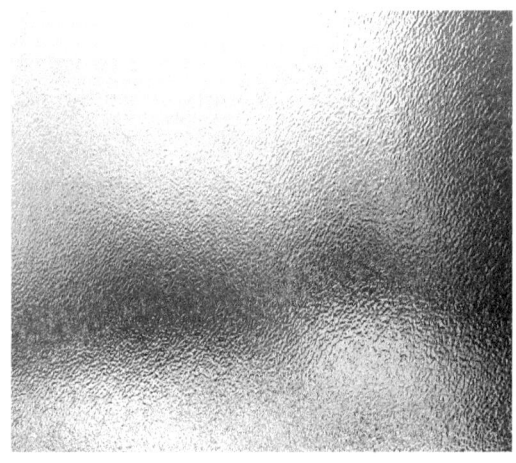

51. interviewer

52. new visions, new practice

The history of the sciences and arts is a tale of recurrent crises, of traumatic challenges, which entail a temporary disintegration of the traditional forms of reasoning and perception … a dismantling of its axioms, a new innocence of the eye; followed by the liberation from restraint of creative potentials, and their reintegration in a new synthesis.

53. cloud-path

54. rules in art

In art and letters, new methods have always
been considered offensive. What must be
avoided above all is the innate conservatism
of totalitarian rules that can be imposed on art.

55. an image of patience

Patience serves us against insults precisely as
clothes do against cold. For if you put on more
garments as the cold increases, the cold cannot
hurt you; in the same way increase your patience
under great injuries, and they cannot vex your mind.

56. theory of nature

Nature *alters itself* by leaps - consequences of this.
Synthetic operations are leaps:
intuitions - resolutions.

Regularity of the genius -
of the leaper par excellence.

57. perception

…what I paint are objects of the mind expressed through plastic means.

If I close my eyes I can see these objects again, only more clearly than with my eyes open; all the little accidental things about them are removed - that's what I paint.

58. fresh look

In his book *Jazz*, Matisse writes how Renoir had told him:
'when I have arranged a bouquet to paint it, I turn and stop at the side I hadn't planned to paint'.

59. discovering, exploring

Don't impose yourself in your creative work - just discover what surrounds you - it's a much richer source - discover rather than fabricate, this way you're forgetting yourself, but you remain who you are. By doing this you're exploring what you encounter, and you can question it, and attempt to understand it.

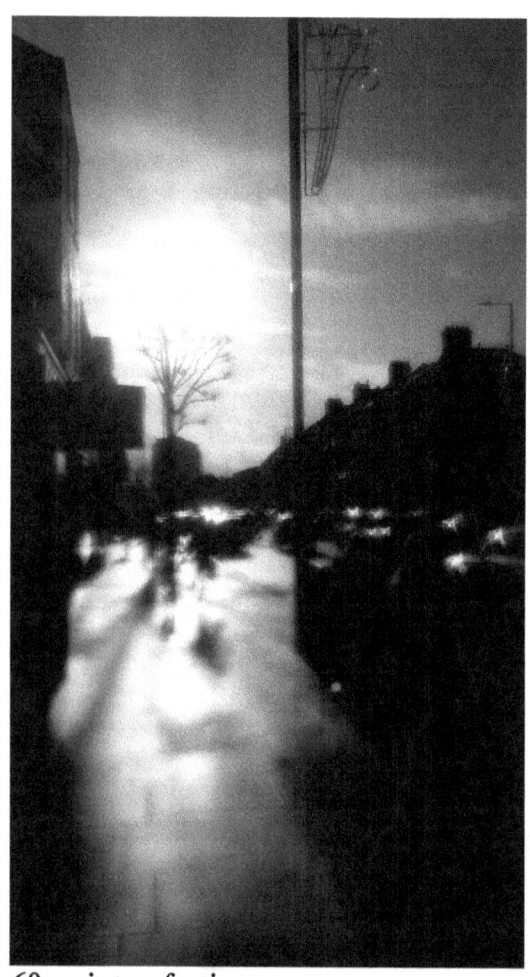

60. winter, festive

61. possibilities?

We enter one of the oldest colleges in the famous, ancient English university, and we both have to bow our heads, as when it was built, people were mostly less tall.

I'm being taken to the Senior Common Room by an academic, before going to lunch with him outside the college, to discuss a publishing project.

I'd read about these Senior Common Rooms - apparently one of their purposes is to encourage a relaxed and sociable mixing of academics from different disciplines, to stimulate a cross-fertilisation of ideas.

But the atmosphere I found in this Common Room wasn't like that at all - it was quite small - the academics were seated in armchairs, lurking behind their newspapers, dominated by a frigid silence. No hint of any greeting for a visitor - it seemed as if everyone there was using their free newspapers to hide behind them.

Evoking a narrow and ultra-competitive world - no doubt these academics had high levels of knowledge and ability within their disciplines, but perhaps a slightly lower level (like their entrance door) of emotional intelligence?

So how would they develop any curiosity about the very different areas being researched by their colleagues?

The possibilities of innovation through the hybridisations of ideas, subjects, or even various approaches, just didn't seem feasible here at all.

So it was a relief to bow our heads once again, and escape into the everyday world of an Italian restaurant nearby, to discuss the publishing project, which sadly was never realised.

At this time, when I was working for an American publisher, I was trying to find an editor for an international series of recordings on DVD, of varied traditional theatre, music and dance from across the African continent, together with accompanying texts exploring these vitally dynamic and influential performing arts traditions.

And as for the newspapers at that ancient college, they were free, as they're part of the concept of the Senior Common Room - presumably they were intended to stimulate discussion.

62. optimism

On this overwhelmingly and
uniformly grey evening,
just look at the warm golden
glow that shines from the
windows in these suburban houses.
A warm welcoming colour,
heightened by the
all-encompassing grey.

63. orders

During lessons, sometimes we heard the shouts of command nearby: the College Cadet Force were doing their drills, marching around the school's grounds.

Then came our turn to be drilled.

We were marched up and down, ordered to move left or right, to avoid marching into a granite wall.

But these repetitions were terminally boring.

How could I evade them?

For me, the vital military uniform saved the day.

It had to be paid for, but my parents, who lived abroad, didn't know about this.

So, fortunately I managed to stay in my civilian school uniform.

I was even given the opportunity of ordering 'my' platoon.

There they were, in full military uniform, their rifles by their sides, in a perfectly straight line, awaiting my commands.

And the school's Resident-Sergeant-Major looked on, in the background, to make sure that all was going to according to plan.

But what would be my first command?

Then I remembered the commanding style, the very loud and penetrating shout, so once I had everyone's attention, I launched into it:

Warayaa-aaaa-shun! (louder) Arayaaraaa-Ha!!

(pause)   Shorrrdaahaa-aa *Hums!*

Total chaos and confusion - nobody in my platoon knew what to do, or even where to put their rifles - they were all over the place.

And it was the end of my possible career in the military line.

But later, I enjoyed shooting.
(that was considered to be a sport, as there were no standard military-style shouted orders).

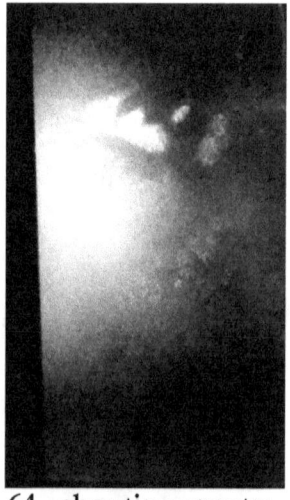

64. shouting spectre

65. another view

He lies on the sand, his head back, and he notices
how people look, as he sees them walking
upside-down. For a moment he experiences
a visual sense of the effect of gravity on
the human body.

66. borrowed solutions

Cartier-Bresson wasn't interested in the new camera
technology - he wants to be able to work with a
straightforward camera he knows well - it provides
a given set of basic possibilities, from which he can
himself choose the one he needs.

This is the opposite of 'pre-sets', the pre-set
decisions on some of today's mobile phones, which
offer built-in recipes provided by others. And which
anyone can follow without needing to think, as the
provision of borrowed thoughts and emotions are
automatically provided.

A basic example of this phenomenon is when you
cannot look at a photograph on a mobile phone in
any way except the 'right way up'!

67. group writing

Some writing group characteristics:

- writers who find it hard to write on their own
- they measure their output, and progress, in numbers of words, and use target word-counts as a stimulus to write
- marketing and placing books into categories is a key topic for discussion
- meetings with decision-makers in publishing, for example editors and agents

  (though these two kinds of jobs are changing, as agents resemble curators more and more, and editors are increasingly concerned just with book production, rather than actually commissioning books and book series)

At one of these writing group meetings (on this occasion there was an agent who had been invited) I asked for some advice - I explained that being awarded an international prize for a book seemed to have caused me more difficulties than any tangible advantages.

There was a stunned silence.

Then one of the writers in the group asked me in disbelief:

'You mean you've won an international prize? ! !'

I nodded.

'Then why on earth are you here?'

I didn't answer, as I felt that the misunderstanding surrounding me was palpable - I even sensed that several people in the group were thinking that I was lying about the prize, as they were looking at me disparagingly, in utter disbelief.

The guest agent kept quiet.

I realised that there was no point in my continuing this discussion - after all, if I'd mentioned the name of the prize, it's very likely that nobody there would ever have heard of it anyway.

But I never did re-visit this group of writers, as I realised that categories and a strict adherence to them was of the utmost importance for them.

Above all, these writers seemed to want to take an active part in a world of writing which has more in common with successfully harvesting a specific crop, hence the importance of target word-counts, plot basics, categories of genres, and related marketing techniques, all of which can be discussed and shared in these writing groups.

On my way out, I heard the guest agent asking an author what kind of book they were writing.

' I'm doing a zombie series for young adults', the author replied.

68. top-drawer

Heard on the radio recently:

'Yes, this is definitely the best performance of top-drawer Bach.'

(But what exactly was in J.S. Bach's *other* drawers?).

69. from the floor

As a result of a meeting at a nearly empty
Café du Dôme in Paris (famous for its
legacy of artists, writers, and poets who
would gather there), I was invited to a
Dada symposium.

A few days later, I found myself in a
sizeable lecture theatre, sitting in the
front row.

The first part of the symposium consisted
of a moderated panel discussion, which
involved a selection of academic specialists
on Dada.

Then, as normal, the chair of the panel
opened the proceedings to questions
from the floor.

And I raised my hand, to ask my first question:

'Ashoniliobata-paplana-woooraaaada-HA!

Irooorodaflenishshks-ks-ks---Haelaidora?

Apapaponishrrrrrda-hhhrrrrrrrO? !

Woorlyiadorrrrma-Hè-Hè-Hè-Hè ! ! ?'

There followed a stunned silence, before
some of the audience began to laugh,
nervously.

I just don't remember what happened after that.

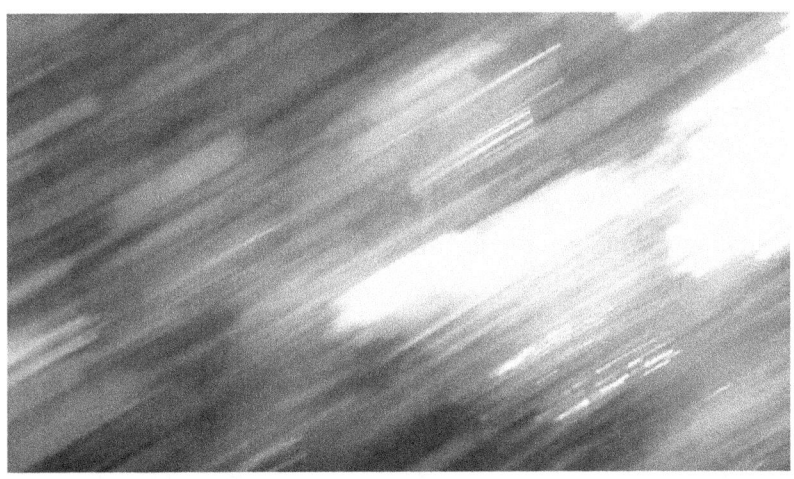

70. dada-speed

71. communications

You mustn't shake hands with people, and certainly *never* say hello to the professors, as they'd just mumble and stumble.

People will initially marvel at the strange behaviour of wild foreigners - how odd they can be, a sort of barbarian - so they must avoid them, and make sure not to recognise them in the street.

The above experience described by Nabokov doesn't only apply to professors.

If you say hello to someone local, you're very likely to be greeted by a stunned silence - this is quite normal, as you first *must* be introduced.

Here is the basic principle which applies:

'we keep ourselves to ourselves, *always.*'

72. silence, power

Nothing strengthens authority so much as silence.

The above reflection (attributed to Leonardo da Vinci) reminds me of someone I once briefly worked with. They never spoke - not that they weren't capable of speaking, they simply chose not to speak - at least this meant that our meetings were always extremely brief, fortunately.

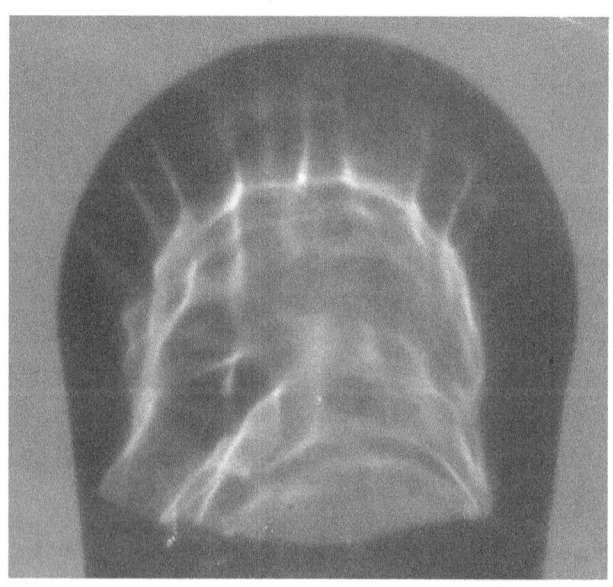

73. commanding presence

74. envy and power

Envy, never dying, never tires of ruling.

75. closed

I first noticed 'Sunday closing'
when I was at school on
the small island of Jersey.
Having grown up in France,
I was shocked by how empty and
desolate Sundays were in St Helier,
Jersey's only town.

On the other days
it was bustling with life,
but on Sunday, everything appeared
to stop. There was nobody
in the streets, no movement, silence
everywhere, just a feeling of static emptiness,
and consequently a threat of boredom,
and depression.

But why did this happen on Sundays?

It was because of the dominance
of the Church. The Church, with its
prayers, hymns, and rituals, dominated
those of us who lived most of our lives
in the school. The extension of its
relentless influence to Sundays, seemed
to me to be an unwanted added restriction.

It successfully promoted in me a lifelong
and continuing avoidance of boring rituals.

And specifically, rituals imposed by authorities,
without reference to any questions.

76. slices of knowledge

The loaves of knowledge do
not come nicely sliced.

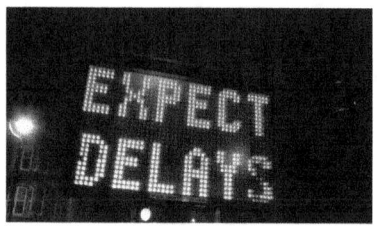

77. clear confusion

78. delays

I've got an interview.
But the streets are full of chaotically static traffic -
the buses are also affected. Apparently this
problem is quite extensive - and it's not clear
what's causing it. As the interview's location isn't
close enough for me to walk there, I now realise
that it probably won't be possible for me to attend
it on time anyway. I enter a shop to find out
what's happening, and if anyone there might know
when the situation is likely to improve.
Nobody really knows what's causing the problem.
The only information they have is that the delays
are really extensive - and the situation is the same
even in the area where my interview is to take place.
I look out through the shop's windows at the lines
of vehicles, immobile in both directions.
There's nothing to be done - for the time being we
are all stuck more or less where we are now.

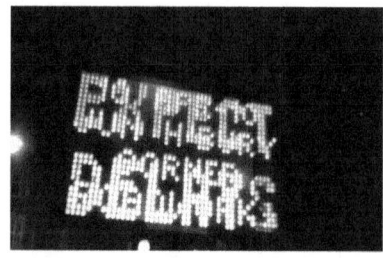

79. mixed messages

80. mechanics of mass power

Power achieved through force, based on a set of fixed inter-related categories:

- religion (the correct one)

- the military (power through unquestioning obedience)

- class (a static concept, whereby there are those who lead, and those who follow)

- the aristocracy (part of a culture which is thousands of years old, based on the ownership of land, and a fixed approach to life, derived from the above three categories).

In summary, everything is based on tradition, on set patterns of thought and behaviour handed down from generation to generation, and maintained in place for centuries.

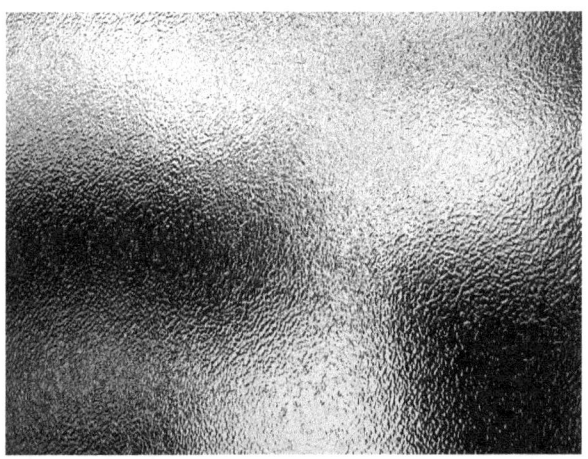

81. unquestioned authority

82. legacies

Here are some examples of legacies that have survived:

- land ownership and its categories, for example freehold and leasehold land.

  This is an inheritance from the aristocracy, still functioning in the UK.

- institutions which maintain set patterns of behaviour, for example the uniform of 'the grey suit', or its equivalent in the business world, an inheritance from the military.

- negative attitudes towards those who aren't from the dominant national culture, and are therefore still considered to be foreign, even though their histories and traditions have become interwoven with the dominating culture - a legacy of being invaded and exploited during past empire-building.

83. an unexpected sense of freedom

I'll never forget the totally unexpected arrival
of the Canadians at my boarding school.

Their accents, their energetic and extrovert ways
were refreshingly different from the rather
reserved manners of the other boys.

For me, aged twelve at the time, these Canadians
were associated with living in vast open and
un-crowded spaces, evoking a much-needed sense
of freedom from the boring collective everyday
rituals of the boarding school, from which others
would occasionally escape, never to be seen
by us again.

Sadly, it's becoming known that many First Nation
children in Canada died in appalling circumstances
at their boarding schools - another terrible legacy
of empire.

84. impossibility

A sea which is a mistake is impossible.

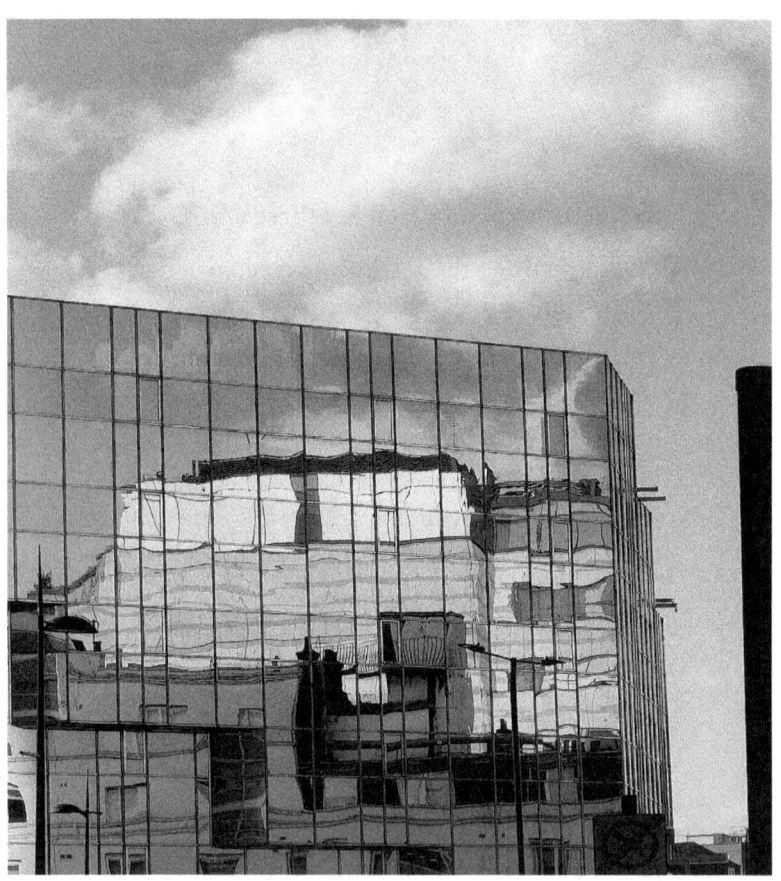

85. reflective

86. for ideas

...look into the rubble of the unconscious and of chance.

87. realisation

...the Aegean has been saying again and again
in the voice of its plashing along an endless length
of coast: *this is you!* And it is repeated by the
shape of the fig leaf against the sky; it is grasped
by the pomegranate that clenches its fist until it
bursts; it is chanted by the cicadas until they
become transparent.

88. applause

Cartier-Bresson's observation that for photographers,
success and recognition are less important than
communication, could also be applied to writers.
But why then are literary festivals considered to be so
important? Apart from the public signings, public
readings and the public presence of the authors
(which will help to sell more of their books) this
marketing approach, involving public approbation,
also inevitably applies to the world of composers and
performers, for financial reasons, and for personal
gratification.
But a problem remains: what happens when there is
applause, but you know that those providing it haven't
the remotest understanding about what you've just told
them or shown them?
And ultimately, does it matter? After all, sometimes you
can understand something only years after you've heard
it - this is probably why Cartier-Bresson places his
emphasis on communication, rather than just immediate
success and recognition.

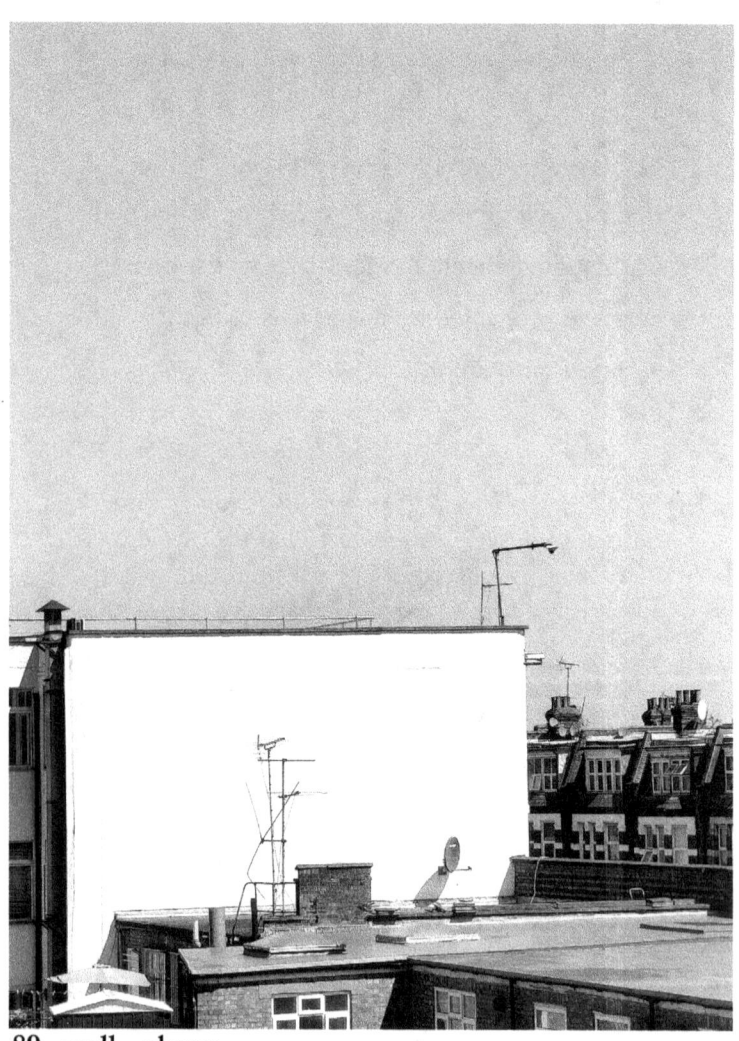

89. wall - above

90. legacy

I don't get any pleasure out of public applause.

My ambition is simply that young people will be able to turn to my books when they feel lonely.

This sort of indirect personal contact, provided it is lasting, is what I consider all-important.

————————————

This approach is opposite to poetry performed to loud applause.

Here is the poet as writer and visual artist, a quieter world of thought, and of impressions, not just hundreds of the audiences' arms waving in unison.

91. sensory pathways

The novel has to go through all the nerve pathways, through your imagination.

————————————

This reflection from Cartier-Bresson brings to my mind Nabokov's statement that he thinks in images - and this includes sound, as in his synaesthetic response to the fish gliding by in an aquarium.

92. reflections

Here are some of the artists, writers and poets Odysseus Elytis met, most of them after World War II, in Paris:

- Picasso, Matisse, Miró, Giacometti, Chagall,

de Chirico, Breton, Tristan Tzara, Reverdy,

Éluard, René Char, Henri Michaux, Sartre,

Camus, Genet, Henry Miller, Allen Ginsberg,

Lawrence Durrell.

His close friend Tériade introduced him to Picasso and Matisse.

(Tériade was from Lesbos, as was the family of Elytis).

The influence of Surrealism on Elytis was a key factor in his encounters with the francophone writers, artists and poets that he met in Paris.

(And Picasso preferred the company of poets).

93. art and language

In his introduction to *Odysseus Elytis, Carte Blanche - Selected Writings*, David Connolly notes that literary critics have tended to ignore the prose writings of Elytis, as they consider his poetry to be more important.

(In the *Greek Poetry Archive* I'd set up, we'd published *The Oxopetra Elegies*, a collection of poems by Elytis, translated by David Connolly).

But then we had a problem: what image should we have on the cover of a book of a collection of the poet's prose? David Connolly suggested a collage by Elytis, a wonderful and appropriate image for this book, especially as the poet was already making collages at the same time as he wrote his first poetry and prose, in the early 1930s.

So for *Carte Blanche*, we included ten of the poet's colour collages, one for the cover, and nine that are featured in the book, which includes a text by Elytis about the freedom his work in collage gives him, to transcribe his poetics to a 'level detached from language's crucifying nails.'

These books were exactly what I wanted to publish: books by artists for artists - books which combine previously separate categories, bringing together more than one medium of expression, in this case to produce inter-reflections between art and language, written and spoken.

In *Carte Blanche*, these means of expression work on the same level, producing unexpectedly magical interactions between the texts by Elytis, and his collages.

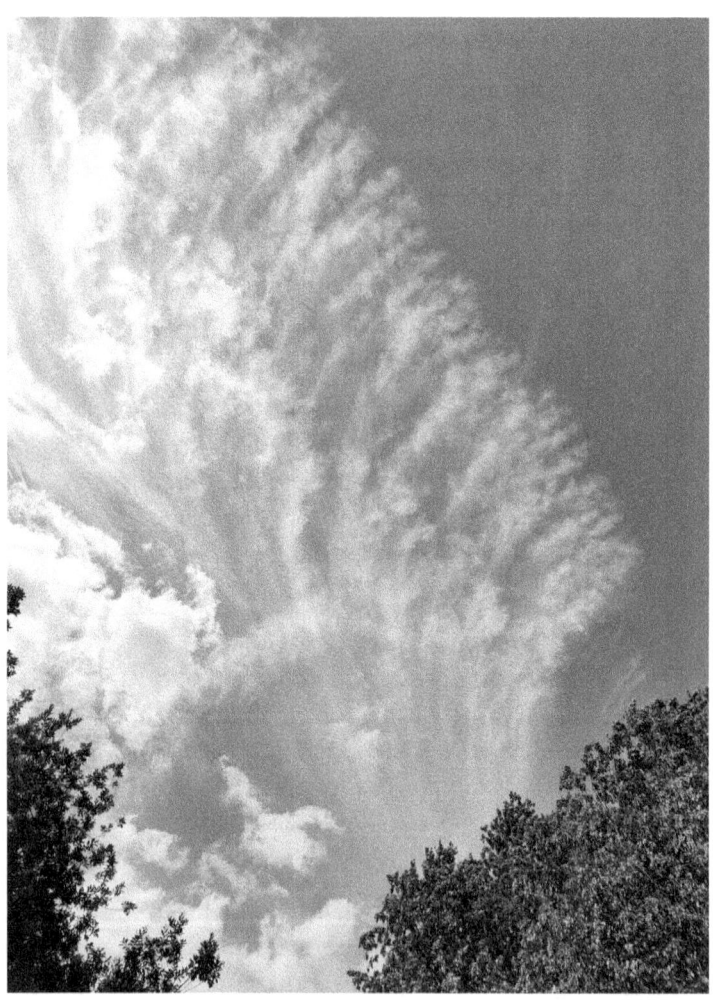

94. vast energy

95. becoming

    All becoming is based on movement...

    for space itself is a temporal concept.

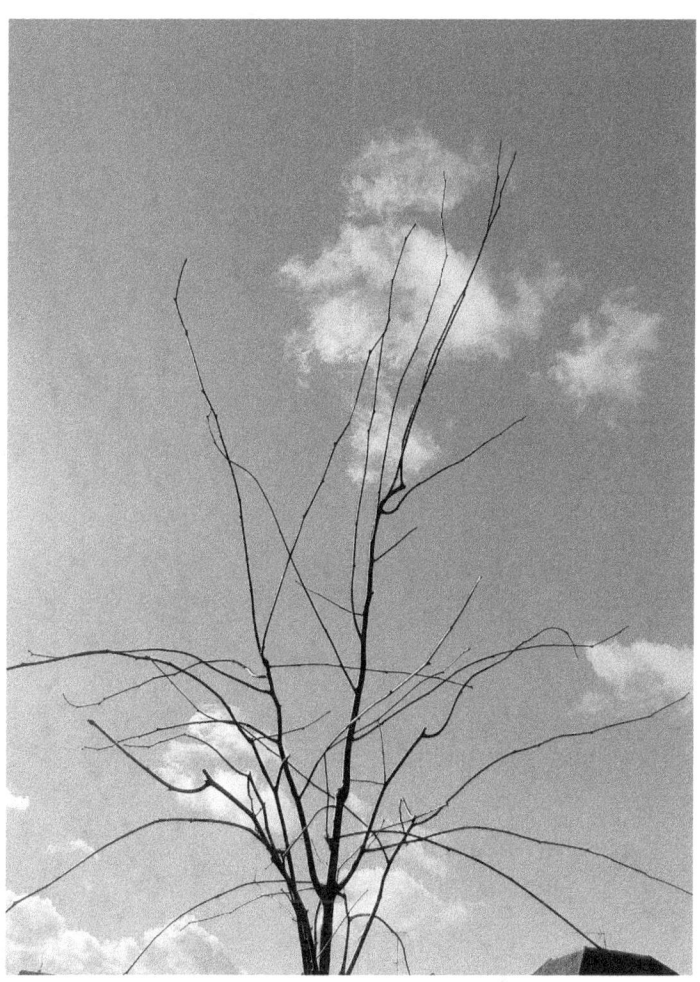

96. interweaving motion

97. waves of time

What we perceive as the present is the bright crest of an evergrowing past and what we call the future is a looming abstraction ever coming into concrete appearance.

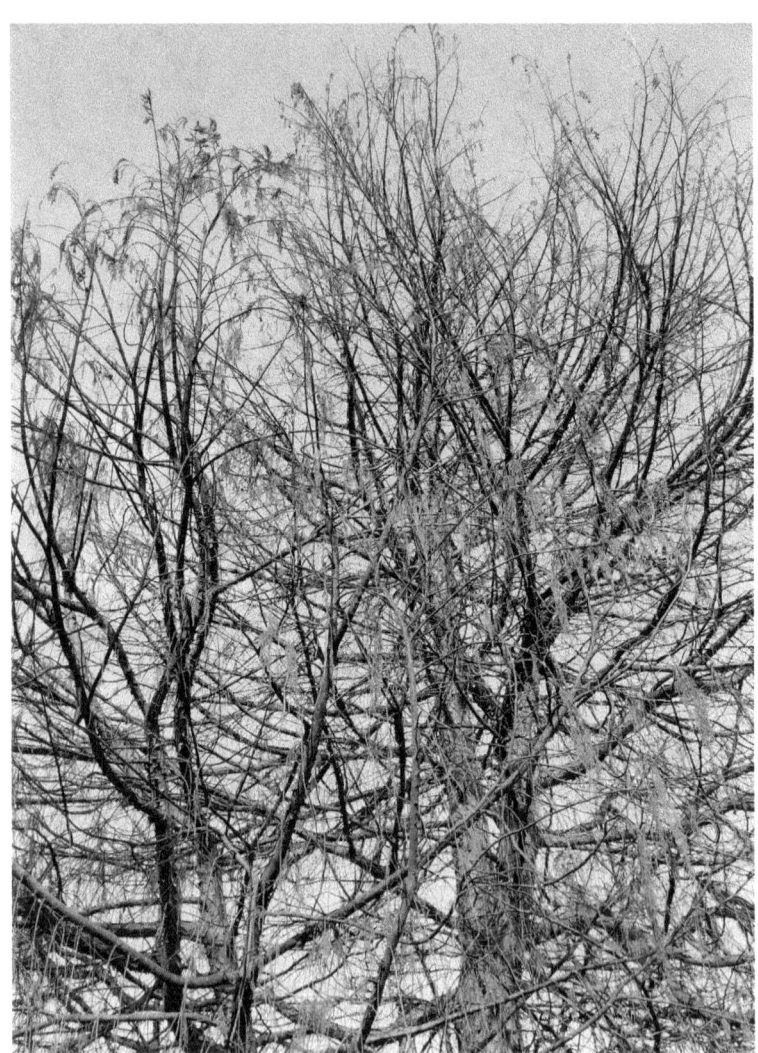

98. energy of interwoven curves

99. motion, abstraction

Abstract formal elements are put together like numbers
and letters to make concrete beings or abstract things.
Here Paul Klee's statement about art also applies
to writing, to mathematics, and to nature.

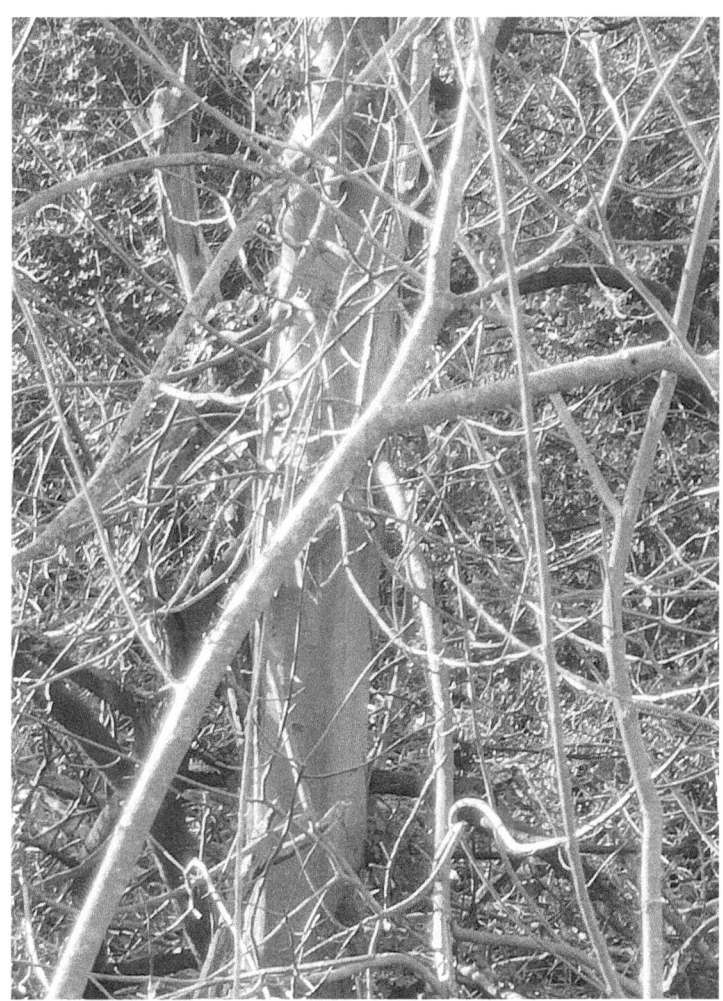

100. interwoven sunlight

101. finding analogies

I have always been preoccupied with finding the
analogies between nature and language in the realm
of the imagination.

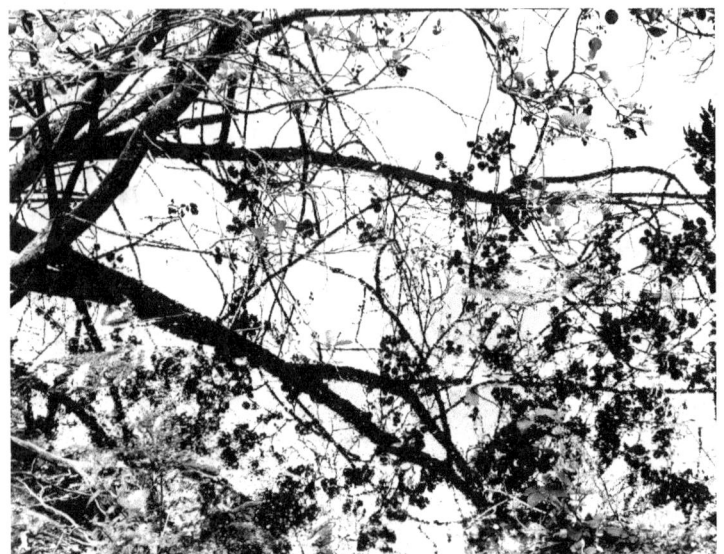

102. reflection on water

103. When we read and hear true poems,
we feel the movement of nature's
inner reason and, like its celestial
embodiment, we dwell in it and
hover over it at once.

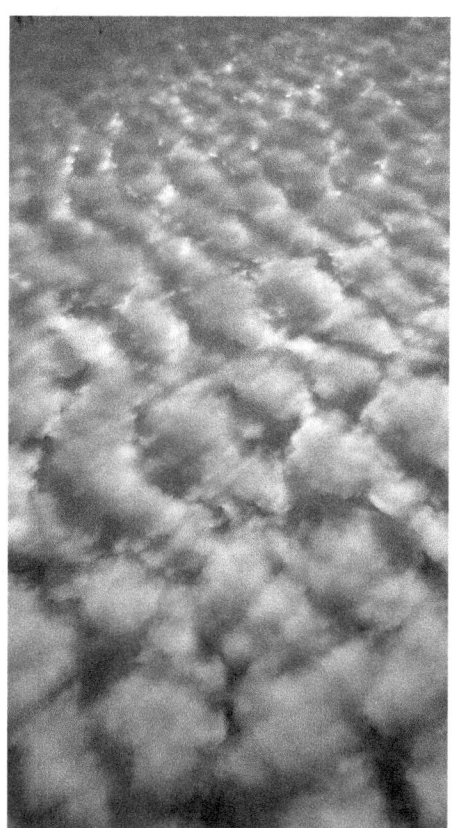

104. interweaving

105. connections

Everywhere he found the familiar,
    only strangely mixed and coupled,
    and thus strange things often ordered
        themselves within him.

Soon he became attentive to the
    connections that are everywhere,
    to meetings and encounters.
        It was not long before he
    ceased to see anything by itself.

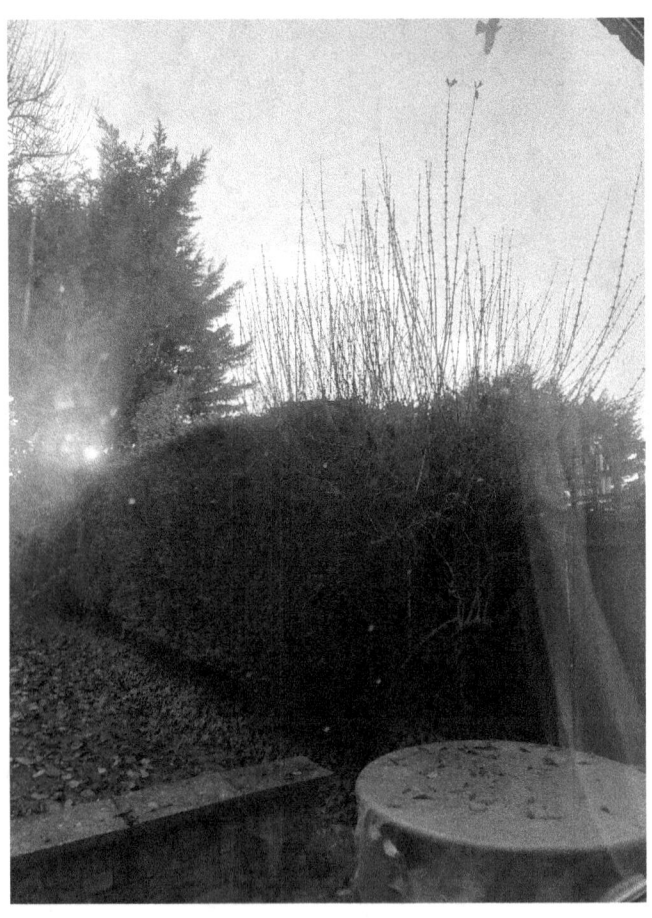

106. big perspectives

The vast view: multiple levels of time, including flight.

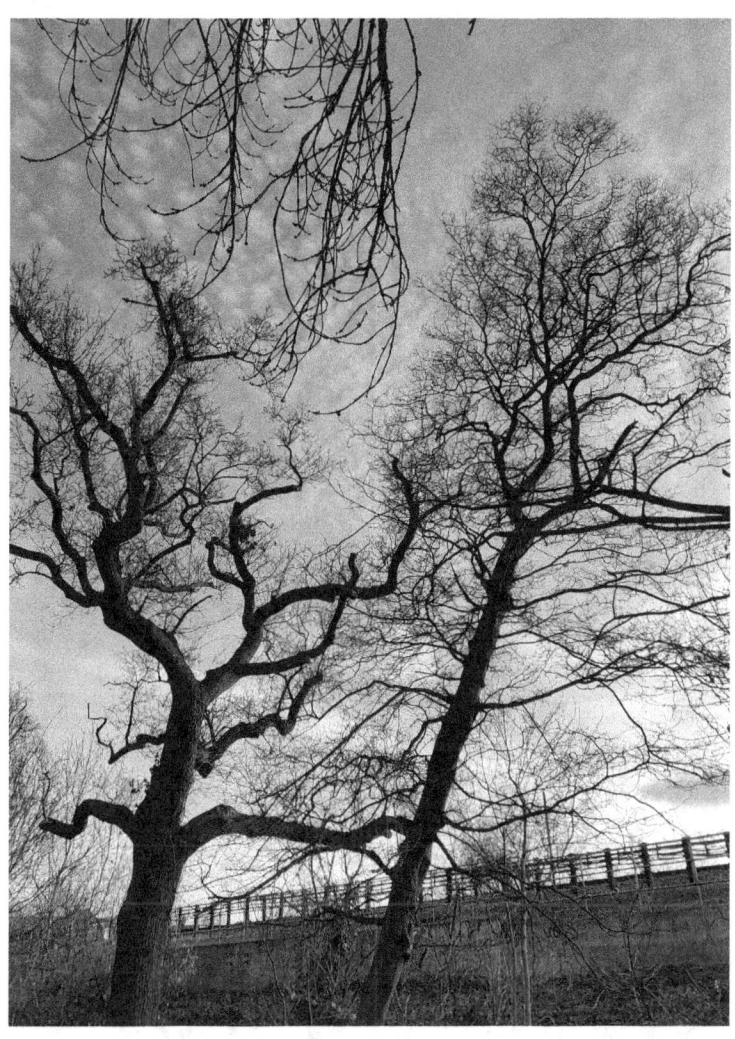

107. lively dancing, evening

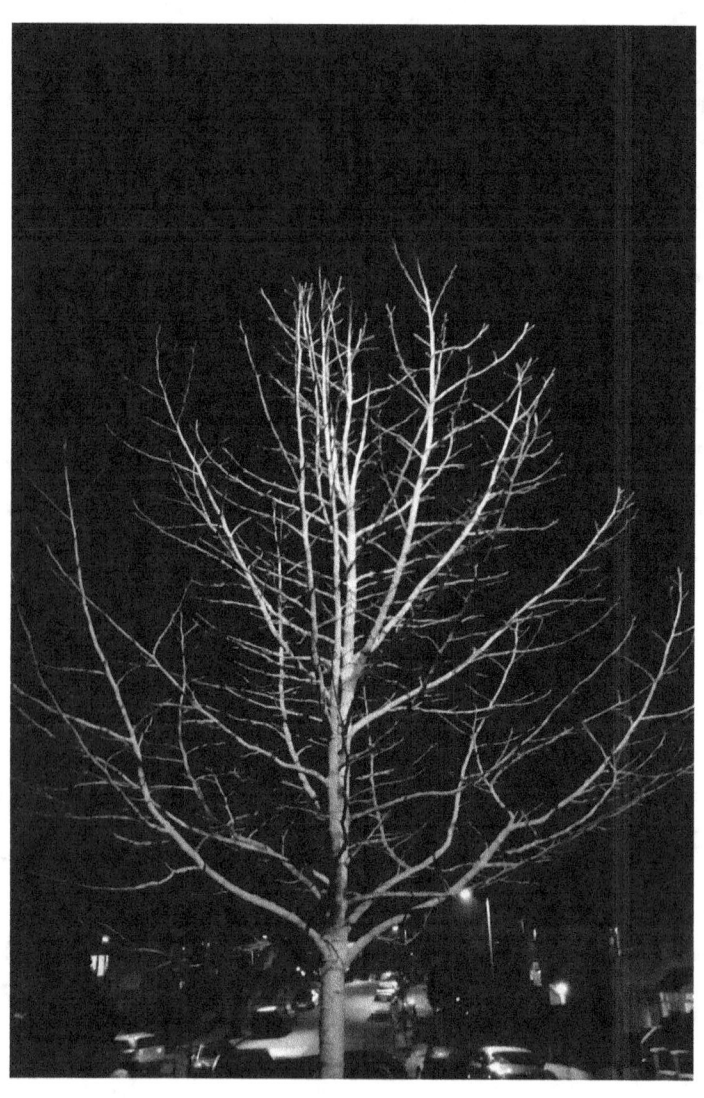

108. night-lights in winter, and the illuminated

109. how to start

When asked about how he starts a novel,
whether it's with a character or a story,
he replies that he begins with neither of
these things - what stimulates his writing
are 'colours, pictures, visions'.

This is why he doesn't begin at the
beginning, or end at the end - and he
never proceeds chronologically.
Instead he starts anywhere, then shifts
to somewhere else to write a very different
image, then he fills in the holes between
these fragments.

Nabokov's description of his writing process
resembles what he does when butterfly-hunting.

110. committees

I *never* had useful editorial committee meetings
for my publishing programme.

All meetings with my colleagues were
one-to-one,
or as needed when a problem came up.

Less frequent were meetings with an author,

an editor, a proof-reader, a printer, also usually

one-to-one - and we always got on together,

as the work was mutually beneficial.

And a lot of work was done, unlike during
the all-day editorial committee meetings with
my science editor colleagues - how could they
be interested in contemporary music, dance and
theatre? It wasn't their fault - they were the
innocent casualties of their narrow
'science *versus* arts' 'focussed' education.

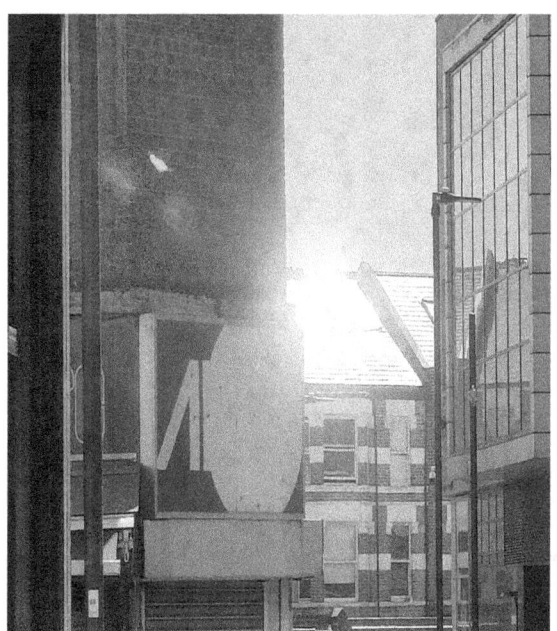

111. methodology

112. 'ology'

The 'ology' added to 'method' is the
warning sign that an academic
approach is ominously
imminent.

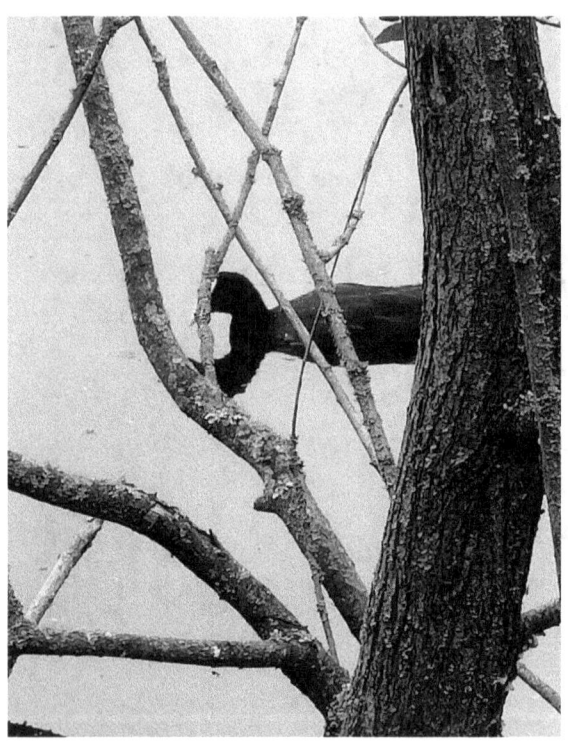

113. unexpected reflection

114. irrational standards

Mixing metaphors is not a problem: he affirms
that he can do this deliberately, as the path of the
'secret connections' between these metaphors
enables him to achieve the positive first step in
the 'defeat of common sense'.

And he defines common sense as
'sense made common'.

All is reassuringly made cheap by its influence.

It inhabits the world of the cliché, where the development of thought disappears in a faithful replication of ready-made and fixed ideas.

What he calls 'irrational standards' (which are the opposite of common sense) have these specific characteristics: the dominance of the detail over the general perception:

- how a part of something will have a more vivid and energetic quality than the whole.

- the way one can observe and acknowledge something small and generally unnoticed by the crowd (a mass of people following a commonly agreed aim, understood by them to be common sense).

Nabokov was making these points in a talk he titled *The Creative Writer*, which he wrote in 1941 - he reminds his audience that 'something called Hitler is trying to turn the globe into five million square miles of blondness and boots'.

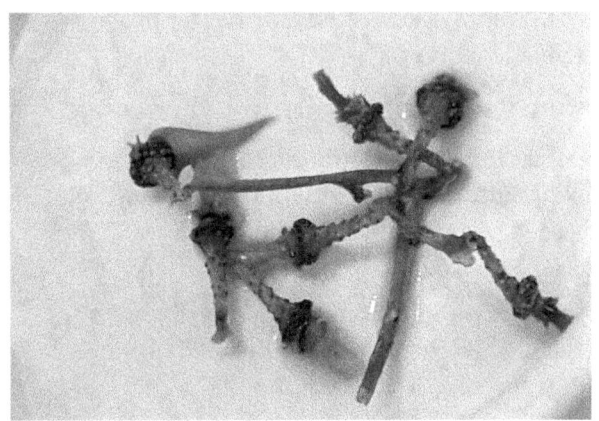

115. jivin'

116. mixed metaphors

The hearts
That spanieled me at heels, to whom I gave
Their wishes, do discandy, melt their sweets
On blossoming Caesar, and this pine is barked
That overtopped them all.

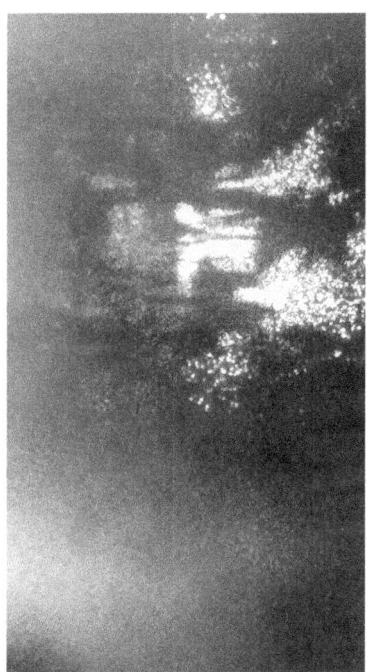

117. nocturnal

118. magazines

'Magazines end up wrapping French
fries, while books remain'.

119. blurry/sharp

Whether a photograph is blurry or whether
it's in sharp focus, its quality depends on
proportions, on the ways black and white
are related in it. In order to achieve these
relations, Cartier-Bresson explains that he
uses 'a spirit of geometry' - this comes into
play when he intuitively knows that he should
at that specific instant capture in a photograph
what is there, before it just disappears and will
never be seen again.

Briefly he has a sudden awareness of the entire
visual structure of what he sees before him,
through his camera's frame. It's there for just
a fragment of a second, a vital and visually
rhythmic part of this fleeting moment that he
has just captured. During this very brief
moment he's holding his breath for complete
stillness, and his heart and head, and
of course his eye, are all involved, simultaneously.

For Cartier-Bresson, art is in the humanity of
your thinking, how you look at things, and the
coincidence of being in a certain place at a
certain time.

120. really travelling

Memories of the day train
from the Gare de Lyon, Paris -
an escape to the Midi,
for the summer holidays.

Our arrival at Tarascon -
Now we have really reached
the South!

The train's windows are pulled
down, the scent of the
sun-warmed herbs from
the *garrigue* fill the compartments,
the light is now noticeably
much brighter, and you can clearly
hear the loud stridulation
of the cicadas.

Everywhere you can see the
tuiles romaines, the red ochres of the
Roman tiles on the roofs of Tarascon,
the southern town made famous
by Alphonse Daudet's account of
the exploits of his comical local
huntsman-hero, *Tartarin de Tarascon*.

And next, you see the distant line
of the Alpilles, the pre-Alps, which are
there on the horizons in paintings
of this region, by Vincent van Gogh.

And it is confirmed that
you have arrived in the Midi,
as the *cuisine méridionale* appears -
the colourful Spanish-style chicken stew
at lunch in the train's restaurant,

as at last you reach the
Mediterranean Sea, then Marseille.

And, at another time, the delicious
fresh garlic-and-olive-oil-rubbed
pan bagnat, sold through the train's
windows, at Aix-en-Provence.

But years later, on a summer business trip,
I fly to Marseille.
And all of these vivid experiences,
the arrival in the South, the scent of
sun-warmed herbs, the Roman tiles,
the change to bright sunlight,
the cicadas, the Mediterranean food,
the landscapes and architecture
which inspired the literature and
paintings of the Midi region -
all of this is totally absent
from the flight.

Travel slowly -
travel all day, all night,
enjoy the multiple sights,
sounds, scents, tastes.

Sadly, it's no longer possible to
open the train's windows, on the
day train to the Midi.

Now the carriages
are air-conditioned,
and the scent of the
sun-warmed *garrigue*
has been replaced
at Tarascon by the rotten egg
stench from a paper factory.

And the varied landscapes
whirl past in a blur.

The previous clarity,
and the glorious
multi-sensory experiences
have gone!

You are dashing as if
to the next business
meeting -
which could be anywhere!

And you are simply
in transition -
you are no longer

really travelling.

121. recollection

...the distant past is highly
organised poetry, the
recent past is nothing
but rough topical prose.

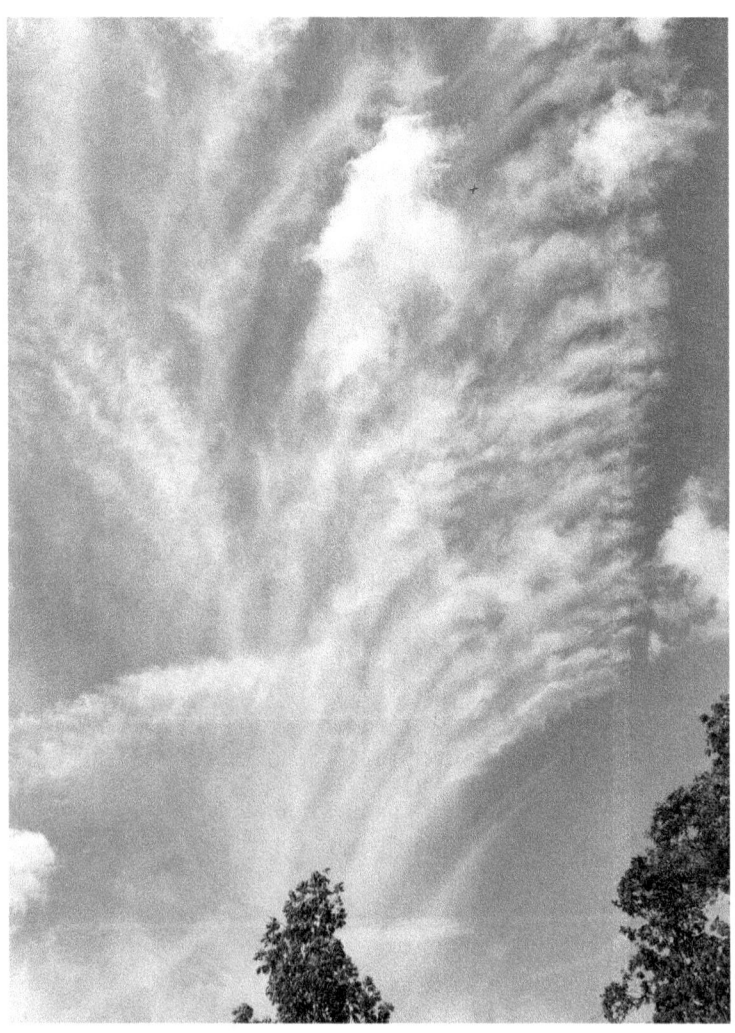

122. energetic, and top right, a jet

123. hunting with Cartier-Bresson

'Concentrate, think, watch, look and hop, like this, you are ready.'

This is like Nabokov when he hunts butterflies.

Cartier-Bresson wants to be as precise as possible, to create abstraction from nature, as in photography, as in science, to discover the world's structure - to enjoy the sensual delight of shape.

This is also a quality Nabokov has, in his scientific study of butterflies, which includes his amazements at their astonishing kinds of camouflage.

124. the favourite photo

Cartier-Bresson mentions how some people ask him which of his photos he likes the best.

This approach is based on the scholastic method of marking homework and essays, which is extended in the academic approach, and also in athletics, where a single person is normally a winner.

But he's not interested in that single winner approach at all: he is already thinking about his next photographic venture, as 'each new project must be approached as a new experience.'

For him, his former achievements are just that - they are part of the past - they don't count, as he has to question everything anew for a new project: it's only by using this approach that he can keep a 'fresh eye' in his work.

This approach is very important - take composers who are caught in one way of working, which they never challenge in their next work.

For example, they continue working with a strictly atonal, or a minimalist approach.

Their contemporaries are working in either one of these styles, so they also impose the same limits on their own work, as their main concern is to follow what others around them are doing, an approach similar to racing.

Cartier-Bresson avoided flying.

His method demonstrates the importance of being open - of not shutting yourself away in tried and tested methods, but being aware of what's around you, of exciting new possibilities which are always waiting to be discovered, instead of hiding in your protective mental tent all the time.

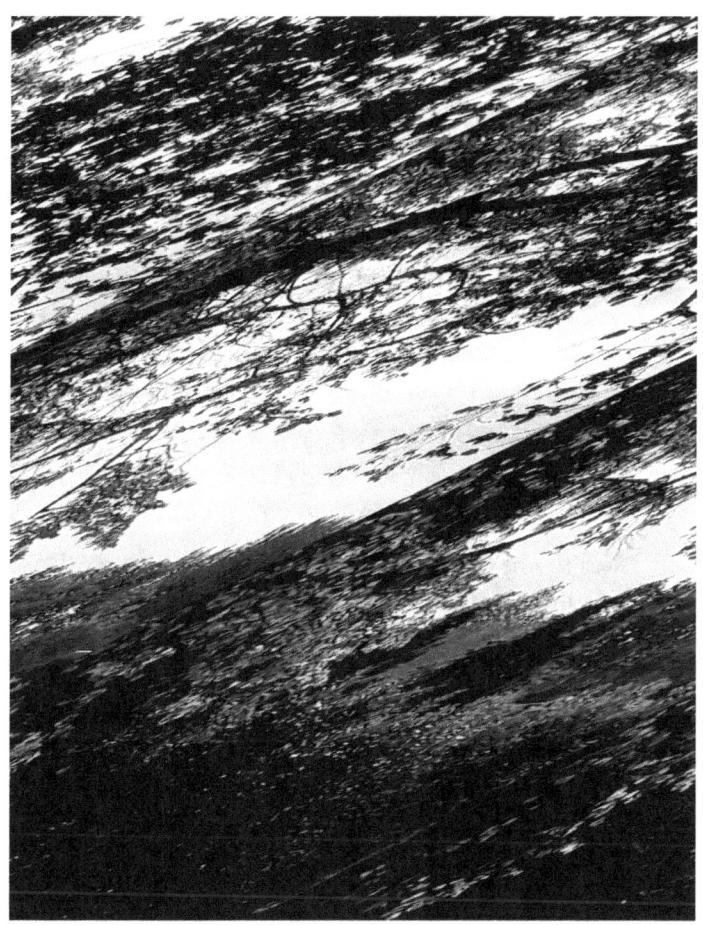

125. evening light

126. imprisoned

An artist must never be a prisoner of herself/himself, a prisoner of a style, a prisoner of a reputation, a prisoner of success...

127. an auspicious meeting

Rufus Collins, the American theatre director and choreographer, invited the Head of London's Society of West End Theatre (SWET) to fly to Amsterdam to attend a performance of my opera *The Kingdom*, which was sold out at the Engelenbak Theatre in Amsterdam.

Rufus, after four months of directing workshops and rehearsals, was now directing the performances of the opera - and he met with the Head of SWET at a restaurant, after the Head had attended a performance.

I wasn't invited - Rufus had directed a successful musical in London, and had also performed in one, so his work was already known to the Head of SWET.

And the next evening, my meeting with the SWET Head was very brief: no convivial aspect to it, not even sitting down.

We stood somewhere in front of the empty entrance to the theatre, as a performance of my opera was in progress.

The first and only thing the SWET Head informed me about *The Kingdom* was that it was too long for a West End production - I would have to cut it.

Of course for me this was an extremely disappointing response - after all, it was my first opera, and it had sold out for every performance, with standing ovations every night.

It was also the most successful production that Rufus had directed in Amsterdam, so this meant that the nature of his own future (as well as mine) depended on the outcome of his production of *The Kingdom*.

But there was also another aspect to the Head's provisional acceptance of *The Kingdom* for a production in London's West End: I knew that if it was insisted that Rufus cut parts of the opera, this would inevitably lead to a work that would no longer belong to my original conception of it.

This was because I had *never*, when composing this work, been influenced by musicals.

The only musicals I liked were the American ones on film from the 1930s, and since then, musicals in London and New York were of course not like these at all - they had become more formulaic.

And with *The Kingdom* I'd composed a new type of opera, most emphatically one which doesn't belong to the existing models of most operas and most musicals: these are categories of works which don't apply, as I'd never intended *The Kingdom* to be either a musical, nor an opera which would need to be performed in an opera house.

But how could I explain this to the Head of SWET?

After all, he was Head of a theatre world in which these categories are, and continue to be, of supreme importance.

So I simply told him that I wouldn't be prepared to make any cuts.

This way I wasn't critical of the production that Rufus had so successfully set up and directed (after over sixty workshops and rehearsals), and I also avoided the possibility that the basic aims of my work would be completely disregarded, so that it would join the legions of standard West End musicals, belonging to an acknowledged, recognisable and predictable category of a product.

The Kingdom has never been performed since its first production in Amsterdam, and its sold-out tour of Holland in 1984 (apart from in The Hague - traditionally conservative).

It was the most publicly successful of my operas.

But just like my other two operas, *The Cathars* and *Empedocles* - *The Kingdom* doesn't fit into the existing categories of what influential people (who often think in pre-existing categories) believe that operas should be like.

For example, for each of these operas I had done much research before writing the libretto, which for *The Kingdom* was my vital six-week research trip to Haiti (and to the Languedoc region in South-West France for *The Cathars*, and to Sicily for my dance opera, *Empedocles*).

I then wrote the libretti for each opera, which in the case of *The Kingdom*, I drew from Alejo Carpentier's novel *The Kingdom of This World*.

And these three very different libretti form the underlying structure for each of these works.

Traditionally a libretto is written by a writer, then a composer is responsible for the music.

And in musicals, the writers normally also exist in a separate category.

But I had in no way imitated these traditional operatic structures for any part of my opera *The Kingdom*.

So why should I have to substantially agree to have key parts of my opera removed?

So that it would conveniently fit the fossilised fundamentals of traditional opera, or the musical?

In which their writers write the texts, followed by the composers who compose the appropriate music?

And why should one take so much time and trouble, including dismantling a successful work, to fit it into a traditional structure, with all its fixed, long-established details of realisation and production, just in order to replicate an existing standard product model?

Where's the original creativity in that?

Richard Wagner wrote both his libretti and the music for his operas, and he even designed his own opera house for them, in Bayreuth.

But I never followed the Wagner-style vocal delivery, born of the need to be heard over a large orchestral sound. And I don't like at all the vibrato-laden singing style, which distorts the pitches and therefore the harmonies in his music for his operas.

These distortions have become part of the static categories that commonly feature in the sound-world of the productions of his music-dramas, and they also feature an 'operatic' style of singing in most operas, which in addition is also a sonic disaster in opera choruses, with their distorted harmonies, caused by a stack of different vibrato-laden voices, each wobbling around their pitches, to a continuously different extent.

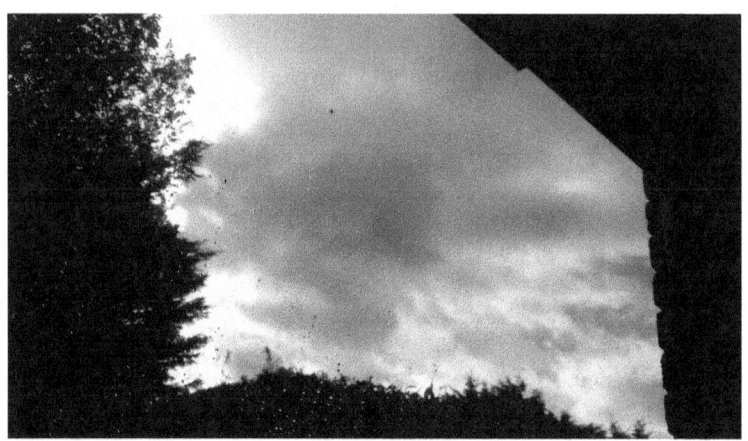

128. high birds fly past on a rainy evening

129. remember that

The poet is always our contemporary.

130. influences

It is only what influences us that is
of importance to us.

131. perception, details, rhythm

When personal vision is involved, there is no

competition... 'general ideas' is a meaningless

concept - small differences, small details are

important - look at Stendhal and small details!

The important thing is to learn how to see, like

composers learn to hear, to listen.

This is vital for something to be expressed,

to be communicated to others.

In photography, in writing, dance, painting,

sculpture and music: in these varied means

of expression, time and space are united -

it's a joyous moment when this

happens: as within the surrounding chaos,

a rhythmic order has been discovered.

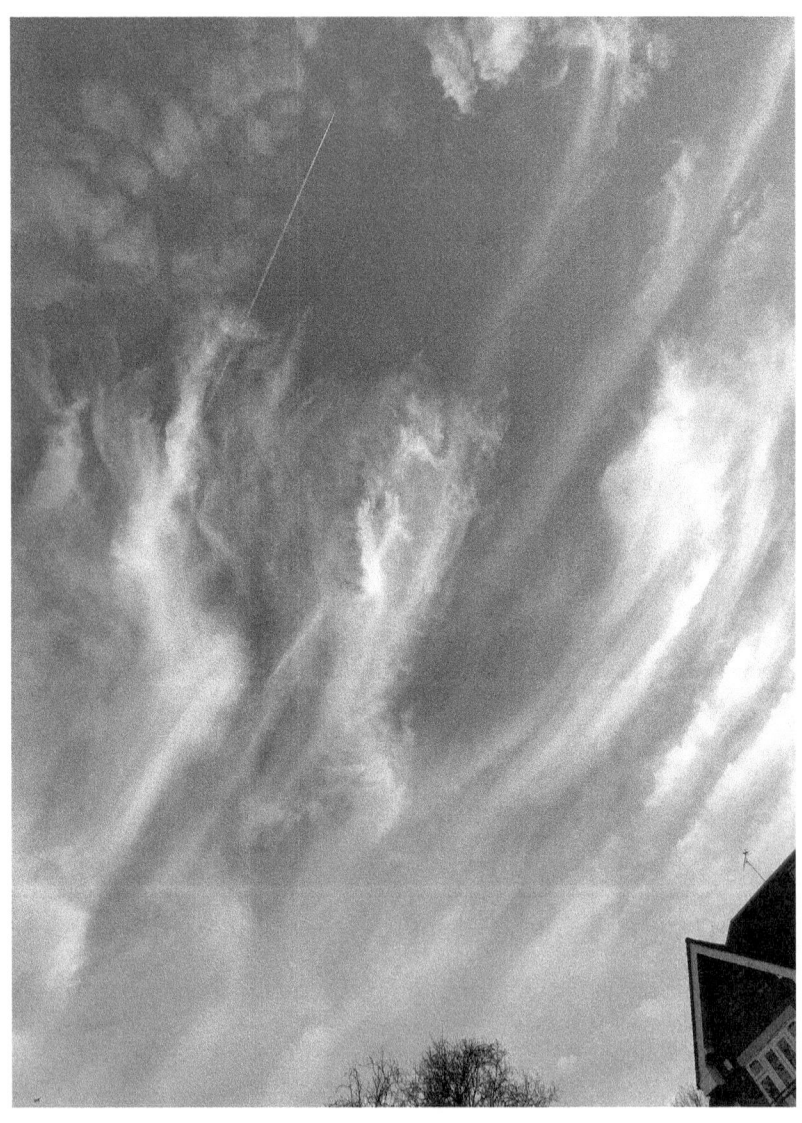

132. upwards - illusory

133. new subjects, new challenges

For the genuine artist, each new subject involves a new challenge, and to triumph over it, all that has been previously learned is irrelevant.

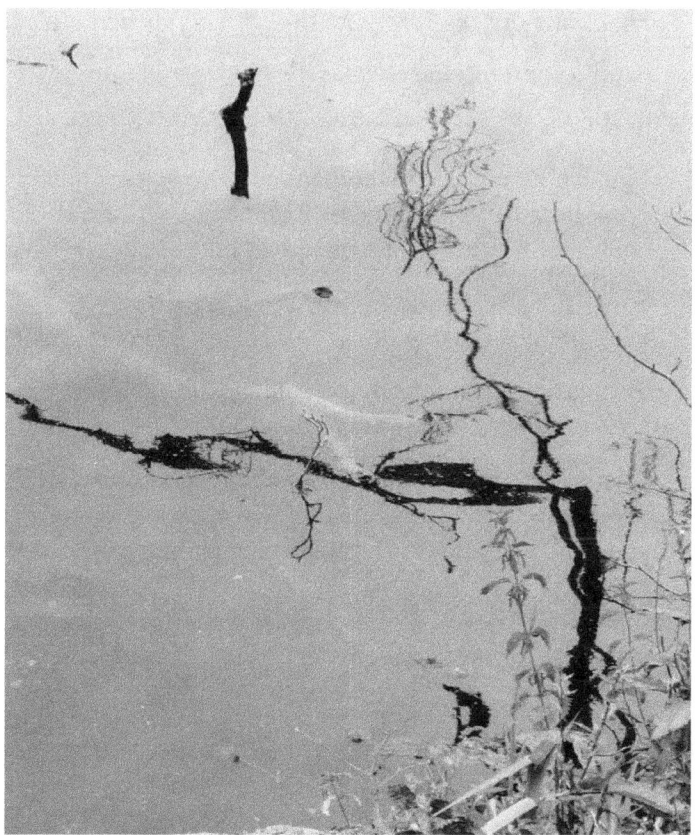

134. reflective games

135. art and the state

Aimé Maeght was astute in his understanding of the relationship between artists and the state.

He points out that the state finds it very difficult to handle contemporary art, as it's not its function to do this - instead its role is to 'conserve and teach.'

I have noticed this phenomenon, when state funding bodies are faced with the problem of how to fund contemporary artists, in any medium.

So what is the solution? You see lots of funding being made available to train young aspiring artists.

The result is that art schools and writing courses and music schools are funded.

That's fine, but it's not by providing a good protégé, or a being faithful disciple that will necessarily stimulate the student to create exciting new work.

You can't grow artists like plants.

136. time-frames

Years ago, I photographed the spring
on a sun-filled blue-sky day.
It's a view from outside Kenwood House,
looking down at the spring flowers
amongst the still-wintered leafless trees,
yet with people lying on cloths
spread on the grass, framed by the
branches in the foreground.
Some are standing,
looking at the view, others
are chatting to each other.
And partly obscured by branches,
at the lower edge of the photo,
is the face of a woman
looking across to the view
to the left, behind me,
her glance at the scenery
caught uniquely across time.

Each person's very different instant
is held in one photographed view,
of multiple views, a picture of
multiple glances, time-frames,
in the present and reflective past,
to possibly become memories,
registered, recorded, as one
overall instant.

137. concentrated awareness

When you press the shutter, you also paint yourself…
to be yourself is also to be outside yourself -
you reach yourself by plunging yourself into the
outside world… photography means concentration.

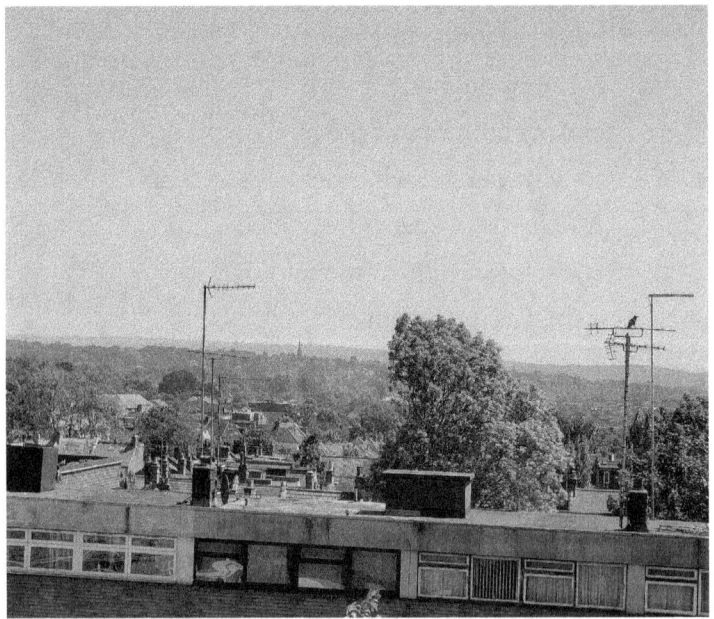

138. a bird views

139. passing years

With age, art and life merge.

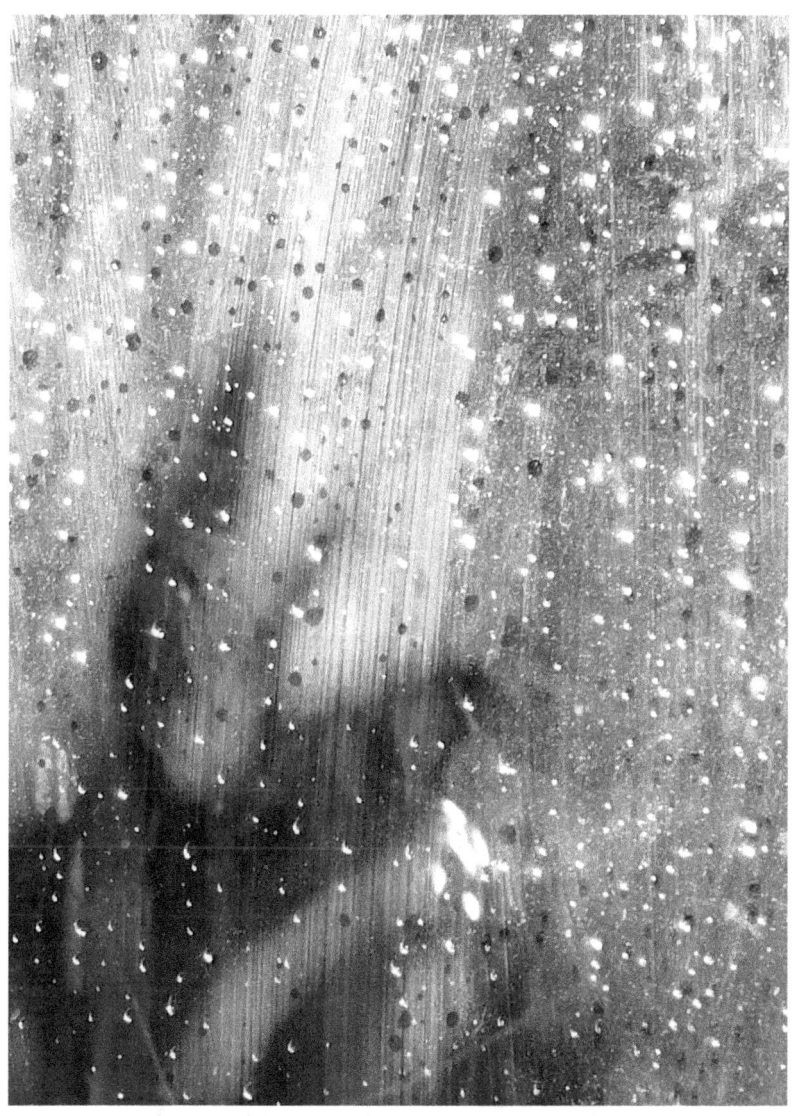

140. cascade

141. art, music, dance

The Marguerite and Aimé Maeght Foundation was made possible due to their close and long-established collaboration and practical working partnership.

It opened in July 1964, with a speech by the writer and culture minister André Malraux, at a crowded opening celebration, with performances by Ella Fitzgerald and Yves Montand, at the inaugural dinner.

Marguerite and Aimé's son, Adrien Maeght, set up the Maeght Foundation Nights in 1965, which over the years presented contemporary music and dance performances, featuring music by a wide variety of living composers.

They included music by Xenakis, Sun Ra, Boulez, Duke Ellington, Stockhausen, Sam Rivers, Messiaen, Terry Riley, John Cage, and modern dance by Merce Cunningham and his dance company, which he had founded at Black Mountain College in 1953.

Sets for these dance works were designed by Jasper Johns, Robert Morris, and Frank Stella. Joan Miró designed the costumes and masks for the production of the satirical *Mori El Merma*, in collaboration with the artist and director of La Claca, Joan Baixas.

These performances reflected Aimé Maeght's early studies at the Conservatoire de Musique in Nîmes, and at the same time training as a lithographer and printer at the École des Beaux-Arts nearby, and setting up a jazz band and performing at local festivals - altogether a truly audiovisual education.

And also vitally important, he had an open approach to art, music and dance, and a fervent desire to combine them in innovatory ways.

142. understanding painting

Don't try to understand painting.

Just enjoy allowing the eye to live its life.

In his wallet, Aimé Maeght carried a copy
of this statement by Claude Monet.

(And of course, it also applies to dance,
and music, audiovisually, and to poetry).

143. creativity

Only combine, but do it in a stimulating and
open way.

144. beyond the proscenium arch

Complete flexibility - this idea describes the practical
approach that Erwin Piscator and Walter Gropius
agreed should be vital for the design of a modern
theatre.

Gropius had founded the Bauhaus in 1919.

In 1926 he had been so impressed by a theatre
production by Piscator, that he'd gone back-stage
to meet him.

They got on very well, and they found that they
shared the same ideas with regard to theatre design.

Shortly after their meeting, Piscator commissioned
Gropius to design the Piscator Theatre.

In his design for this theatre, Gropius was inspired by a memorable experience he'd had at a production directed by Max Reinhardt: at a moment of extreme tension, one of the actors had totally unexpectedly spoken from behind the audience.

Gropius was bowled over by this effect - he felt that he was actually involved in the performance itself.

It was as if the separation between the actors and the audience had suddenly disappeared, so that the audience found itself taking an active part in the production.

Gropius explains that this experience was what he later called 'total theatre', and that it was his starting point for the design of his theatre for Piscator.

And looking at his design, you can see these innovations:

- the actors are surrounded by the audience

- there is space for the performers to act anywhere, including *behind* the audience

- there's a slowly revolving auditorium which can be moved past three stages during a performance

- there are spaces for projecting films as part of the performance, as in Piscator's productions, thus replacing the traditional theatre's mostly static scenery

- the film projectors can be placed anywhere around the audience, which enables the scenery to be screened above and also behind the audience, so that they feel as if they are actually taking part in the performance.

Piscator was delighted with the design that Gropius had devised.

But sadly, due to the disastrous impact of the 1929 financial crash on the German economy, the Piscator Theatre was never built.

Piscator emigrated to the United States in 1939, and in 1940 he was invited to launch the Dramatic Workshop at the New School for Social Research in New York.

Judith Malina studied with Piscator - in her diary in 1948, she describes how he 'creates a stage that one can play on, under or around...the small stage seems to expand: a revolving platform allows cinematic effects of action in motion. Actors walking on a turntable that revolves against them, or single spot-lit faces function as theatrical equivalents of the moving camera and the close-up.' She concludes that Piscator isn't an 'actor's director' but that he is there 'in the style of all the actors.'

The Living Theatre, which she had set up with Julian Beck in 1947, could be effective without the need for the construction of a new, expensive, and specially designed Total Theatre building, like the Dallas Theater Center, which had cost over a million dollars and four years to build.

Frank Lloyd Wright had designed a theatre for the West Coast back in 1915, which was never built. So when he'd been approached to design a theatre for Dallas four decades later, he adapted his original design. This is the only theatre designed by Wright that was ever built, and he died aged 91, just nine months before it opened in December 1959.

Interestingly, his theatre has elements which are similar to the Total Theatre design by Gropius: it has a revolving stage which projects into the audience space, and in addition there are side stages which also add to the audience a sense of actually being part of the performance.

The artist George Grosz produced cartoons and designed sets and costumes for Piscator's stage adaptation of *The Good Soldier Schweik* (1927-1928), the comic novel by Jaroslav Hasek, which is set in the First World War.

Grosz, when writing about Piscator, points out that his friend was constantly searching for a way to realise 'a total art form which would embrace all the arts.'

In 1980, I found the ideal subject for a new form of opera, which I believed would achieve such a total art form: the subject was the Haitian Revolution, which I'd drawn from Alejo Carpentier's novel, *The Kingdom of This World*.

I intended to compose a work that *couldn't* be performed in an opera house, with its proscenium arch and large space for the orchestra, which separates the audience from the action on the distant stage.

I was influenced by Mussorgsky's opera *Boris Godunov*, and inspired by the singing styles from South Africa, Zimbabwe, and Haiti.

So I composed a synthesis of music, dance and theatre, a work in which choral singing is as important as any solo singing.

In addition, I wanted to have natural singing voices, not those voices which make a strong and sonically distorting use of vibrato, so as to be heard above the loud volume of an opera's orchestra.

In *The Kingdom* my orchestra continually changes its size and tone colour and function, as a significant part of my score is recorded, and then projected into the performance space.

And also I wanted to have musicians who actually perform in the area where the action is taking place, and a choir who both sing and move and dance in and around this space.

And so there was no possibility to conceive how my opera *The Kingdom* could be performed in the UK at this time.

However, I was very lucky that Jo Whelan, the Administrator of the Black Theatre Cooperative in London, suggested that I contact the American director and choreographer, Rufus Collins about *The Kingdom*.

We met twice, and on the second occasion I went over the libretto I'd written, based on Carpentier's novel, and I played on the piano some extracts from my score.

Rufus had been an actor with The Living Theatre, and this was something in which I was particularly interested, as the concept of total theatre was a key influence in my aim to create a new kind of opera, which would be effective in a theatre, in which the audience would feel that they were directly part of the action that was taking place around them.

At that time Rufus was working as a director at the Engelenbak Theatre in Amsterdam.

Their staff were looking for a large-scale production, to begin their 1984 season, so Rufus proposed my opera, *The Kingdom*.

It was accepted, and Rufus assembled a cast of 35 performers who he directed in over sixty workshops and rehearsals.

And from the very start, Rufus arranged a detailed plan for his production of *The Kingdom*.

For example, the audience, as they entered the theatre, found themselves entering a lively Haitian market, and they were encouraged to buy the Caribbean fruit on sale there, so they immediately found themselves in the location where the action depicted in the opera was to take place.

Visual projections provided the settings for the various scenes, and the live instrumental and processional choral music, and the dances, and the varieties of projected music, all gave the audience a feeling that they were actually a part of the action, in the historical events that they were directly witnessing.

For Piscator, the history of theatre consists of the varying degrees of success in creating 'the illusion that the audience participated in the play.'

I believe that Piscator's statement about theatre is as applicable to opera, as much as to plays, and any other form of theatre and dance.

It's still vital today to create new kinds of operas, which abandon the aristocratic proscenium arch and the artificially raised stage, in order to enable audiences to find themselves totally involved in the action that is taking place around them.

The total theatre approach was a key factor
in my libretto, and in my music for *The Kingdom*
- it was also central to Rufus Collins' production
of my opera.

And it is truly astonishing that after nearly a
century since the innovations of Piscator,
Gropius, and Frank Lloyd Wright, and
many others - the truly exciting total theatre
approach seems to have all but disappeared!

---

145. skies

Grey sky

low light,

brilliant sky,

blue light.

At any time

you can feel

the weight and the

light of the everyday.

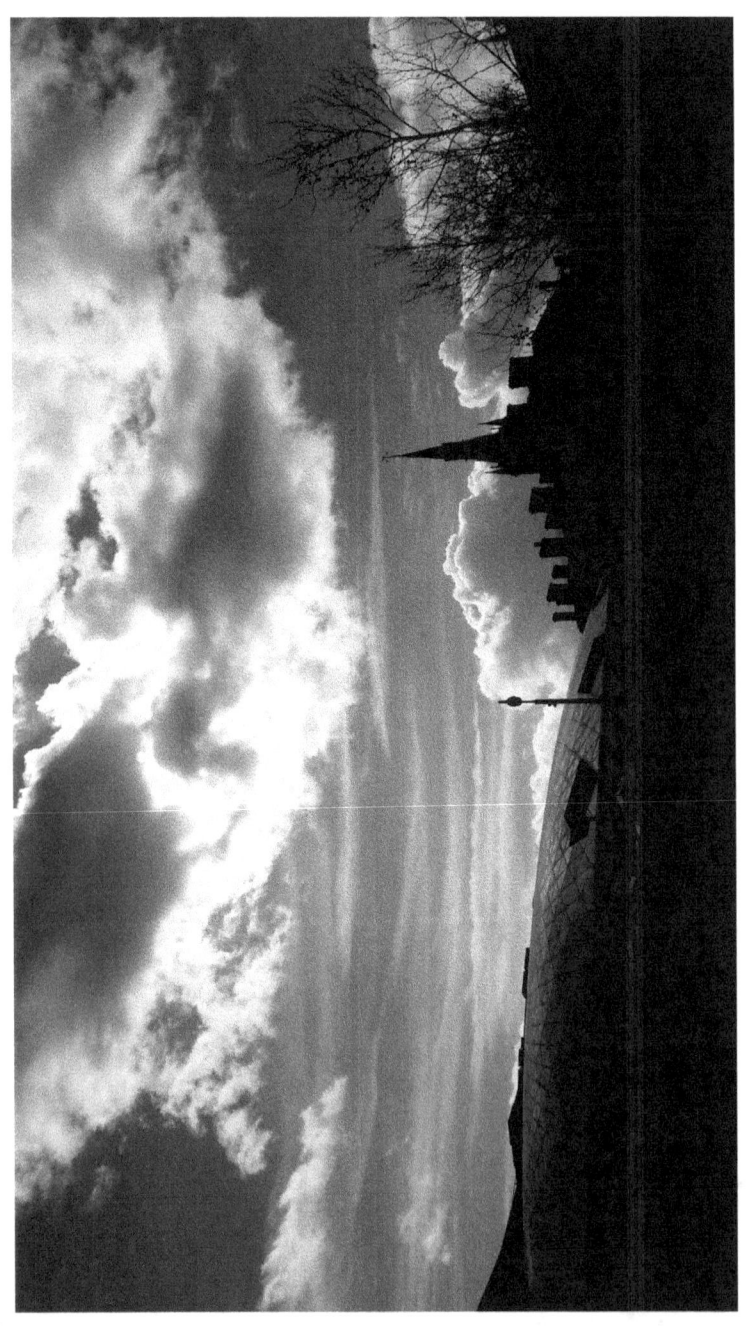

146. Morning

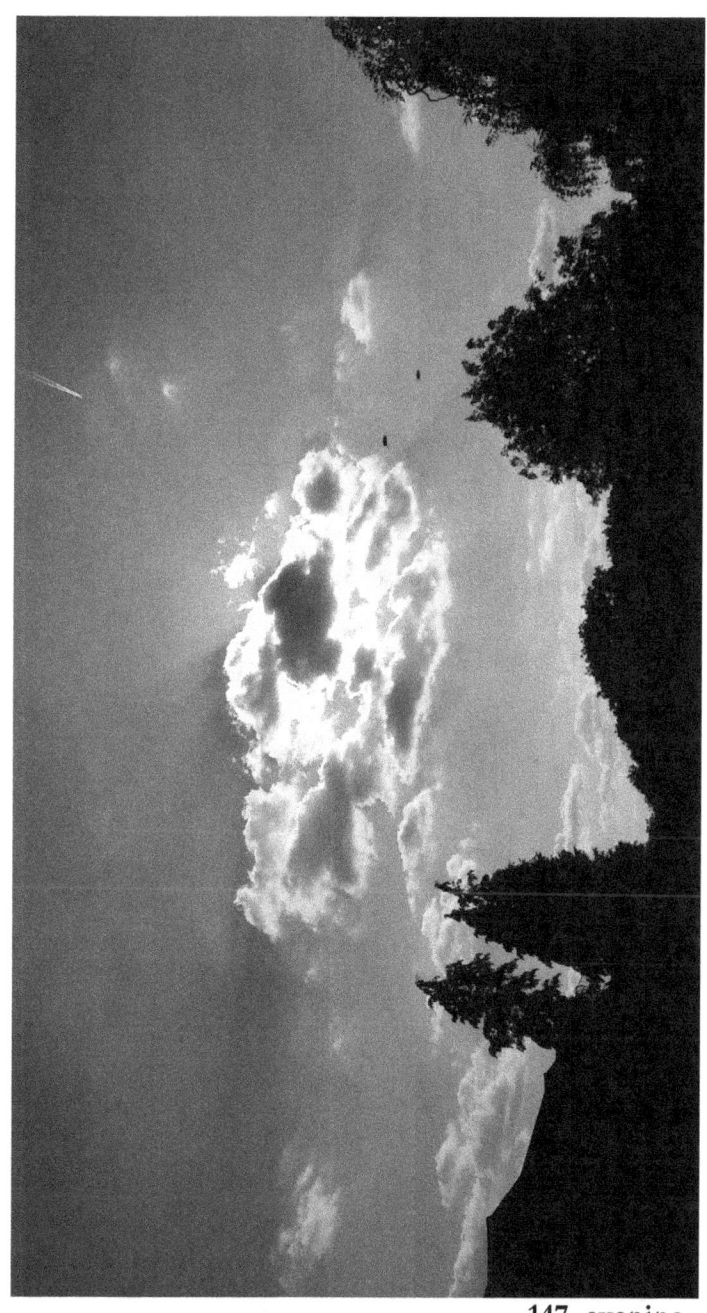

147. evening

117

Page 9, epigraph: *Cahier de Georges Braque 1917-1947*,
   Maeght Éditeur, 1947, p.57.

2. multi-dimensional inspiration
The shared category question inevitably comes up
with these lists: for example Montaigne,
Saint-Simon, and Bakunin are also considered to be
philosophers, and the Buddha is a religious leader.

Henri Cartier-Bresson, *Interviews and Conversations*,
pp.10, 17, 26, 32, 61, 145.

9. precision, inspiration
Vladimir Nabokov, *Think, Write, Speak*, a collection
of various writings, essays and interviews, edited by
Brian Boyd and Anastasia Tolstoy, Penguin Classics,
2019, p.339. My notes.

11. the bigger picture
André Gide, *Conseils au jeune écrivain*, Éditions Proverbe,
Paris, 1992, p.22. My translation.

12. inexplicable
Cahier de Georges Braque 1917-1947, Maeght Éditeur, 1947.
My translation.

14. categorical
An unexpected comment from the English composer
William Walton leads to my exploration of various
innovative combinations of music, texts, and sounds
that break open pre-existing musical categories.
Walton's comment is in *Mahler: His Life and Music*, by
Stephen Johnson, Naxos Books, 2006, p.71.

16. composition by fragments
Vladimir Nabokov, *Think, Write, Speak,*
Penguin Classics, 2019, p.338. My notes.

17. danger
An ancient Chinese proverb.

22. communicating photographs
Henri Cartier-Bresson, *The Mind's Eye*, p.42

25. unreal
Vladimir Nabokov, *Think, Write, Speak,* p.323.

28. humour
Vladimir Nabokov, *Think, Write, Speak,* p. 320.

32. choice from chaos
Cartier-Bresson, *Interviews and Conversations*, p.66.
My notes.

36. generalisations
Vladimir Nabokov, *Think, Write, Speak,* p.50.
My notes.

38. creative legacy
Paul Klee's reflection, reproduced on his
tombstone, in Schosshalden cemetery,
Berne, Switzerland.

39. the nature of poetry
Cartier-Bresson, *Interviews and Conversations*, p.58.

41. realities
Vladimir Nabokov, *Think, Write, Speak*, Nabokov,
p.365. My notes.

43. risk of merit
Johann Wolfgang von Goethe, *Maxims and Reflections*,
Penguin Books, 1998, p.115

44. ordering hierarchies
Cartier-Bresson, *Interviews and Conversations*, pp.64, 151.
My notes.

46. to be aware beyond style
Cartier-Bresson, *Interviews and Conversations*, pp.107, 108.

48. challenging cacti
The quote is from a wikipedia text about cacti.

49. truth in relation
The first two statements are my notes on
Cartier-Bresson's thoughts on truth and the role and
importance of relationships in art and in life.
Henri Cartier-Bresson,
Interviews and Conversations, 1951-1998, p.65.

52. new visions, new practice
Arthur Koestler, *The Act of Creation*, Arkana, p. 461, 1989.

54. rules in art
My summary of Nabokov's warning about
innately conservative art and writing.
Vladimir Nabokov, *Think, Write, Speak*, p.166.

55. an image of patience
From *The Notebooks of Leonardo da Vinci*, selected
and edited by Irma A. Richter, Oxford University
Press, 1990.

56. theory of nature
Novalis, *Notes for a Romantic Encyclopaedia*,
State University of New York Press, translated, edited
and introduced by David W. Wood, 2007, p.28.

57. perception
Matisse, from a conversation with Louis Aragon.
Matisse by Matisse, edited and with an introduction
by Rachel Barnes, 1990, p.64.
Aragon wrote *Henri Matisse, Roman*, the result of
thirty years of his reflections about the creative
approach of artists and sculptors, through
conversations with his friend Matisse, and his
own creative practice as a poet and writer.

58. fresh look
Jazz by Matisse was published by Tériade in 1947
in Paris. George Braziller published it later in 1992.
Matisse's quote from Renoir is on pages 38 and 39.
My translation.

59. discovering, exploring
Leonardo da Vinci.
Cartier-Bresson, *Interviews and Conversations*, p.71,
my notes.

65. another view
Vladimir Nabokov, *Think, Write, Speak*, p.106,
my notes.

66. borrowed solutions
Cartier-Bresson, *Interviews and Conversations*, p.83,
my notes.

71. communications
My notes on Nabokov's experiences as a student
at the University of Cambridge from 1919-1922,
and how little has changed since then.
Vladimir Nabokov, *Think, Write, Speak*, p.5.

74. envy and power
Leonardo da Vinci, in *Leonardo's Notebooks*,
ed. Anna Suh, Black Dog and Leventhal Publishers,
New York, 2013, p.166.

76. slices of knowledge
Vladimir Nabokov, *Think, Write, Speak*, p.221.

84. impossibility
From *Maria Nefeli*, by Odysseus Elytis, 1979.
Translation by Nanos Valaoritis.
From *Odysseus Elytis, Selected Poems*,
chosen and introduced by Edmund Keeley and Philip Sherrard,
Anvil Press Poetry Ltd., 1991.

86. for ideas
Cartier-Bresson explains how Surrealism was an
important influence on his approach to photography -
he knew André Breton, and would attend his meetings,
but he never became a member of his Surrealist
movement of artists, writers and poets.
Henri Cartier-Bresson, *The Mind's Eye*,
Aperture Foundation, New York, 1999, p.98.

87. realisation

From *Draft for an Introduction to the Aegean world*, in
Odysseus Elytis, Carte Blanche, Selected Writings,
translated and with an introduction by David
Connolly, Harwood Academic Publishers, 1999, p.5.

88. applause

Henri Cartier-Bresson, *Interviews and Conversations,*
p.33.

90. legacy

Three remarks by Odysseus Elytis, published the day
after he'd received the Nobel prize for literature.
From Yiva Wigh, *The Wanderings of Odysseus*, in
The Guardian, 19th October 1979.
(Below the line, my two comments).

91. sensory pathways

From Henri Cartier-Bresson:
Interviews and Conversations,
1951-1998 : a conversation with Sheila Turner-Seed
in 1973, featuring an account of the photographer's
creative process.

92. *The Oxopetra Elegies*, Odysseus Elytis, translated by
David Connolly, Harwood Academic Publishers,
1996, pp.79, 80.

93. art and language

Odysseus Elytis, *Carte Blanche - Selected Writings,*
translated by David Connolly, Harwood Academic
Publishers, 1999.

95. becoming.

Paul Klee, *Creative Credo*, 1920

97. waves of time

Vladimir Nabokov, *Think, Write, Speak*, p.470.

99. motion, abstraction

Paul Klee, *Creative Credo*, 1920.

101. finding analogies

Odysseus Elytis, from Adriana Simos, *Remembering Odysseus Elytis, the Nobel Prize-winning poet*, *The Greek Herald*, 19th March 2020.

103. When we read and hear true poems

Novalis, *The Novices of Sais*. Archipelago Books, 2005, p.25. (I read this text after having completed *Vertical Gliding*).

105. connections

Novalis, *The Novices of Sais*. Archipelago Books, 2005, pp.8,9.

106. big perspectives

The window lens - lenses and time. For my continuing exploration of the relation of time and space - with regard to lenses, see *Cinema and the Audiovisual Imagination*, pp.212-217.

109. how to start

Vladimir Nabokov, *Think, Write, Speak*, Penguin Classics, 2019, p.338. (My notes.)

114. irrational standards

Vladimir Nabokov, *Think, Write, Speak*, pp.192-194. (My notes.)

116. mixed metaphors

From Shakespeare's *Antony and Cleopatra*, Act IV, Scene 12. With thanks to poet E.P. (Paul) Guest.

---

118. magazines
Henri Cartier-Bresson, *Images à la Sauvette*,
the Henri Cartier-Bresson website.

119. blurry/sharp
Even after the introduction of colour film,
Cartier-Bresson preferred black and white
photography.
Henri Cartier-Bresson, *Interviews and Conversations*,
pp. 21, 28, 29, 134.

121. recollection
Vladimir Nabokov, *Think, Write, Speak*, p.407.

123. hunting with Cartier-Bresson
Cartier-Bresson, followed by my comparison
with Vladimir Nabokov.
Cartier-Bresson, *Interviews and Conversations*, pp.56, 62.

124. the favourite photo
Henri Cartier-Bresson, *Interviews and Conversations*,
p.32, along with my reflections.

126. imprisoned
Henri Matisse, in Elderfield, John (1978).
The Cut-Outs of Henri Matisse, New York,
George Braziller, p.8.

127. an auspicious meeting
For more information about *The Kingdom*, see
<The Kingdom opera> on the Net.
My book, *A Summer in Haiti* is my account of
my research trip to Haiti in 1981, before
I composed the music for my first opera,
The Kingdom.

129. remember that
Virginia Woolf, *On*, Hesperus Press Ltd.,
2008, p.67.

130. influences
André Gide, *de l'influence en litérature*, Éditions
Proverbe, Paris, 1992, p.62. My translation.

131. perception, details, rhythm
Cartier-Bresson, *Interviews and Conversations*,
pp. 66-68. My notes.

133. new subjects, new challenges
André Gide, *Conseils au jeune écrivain*, Éditions
Proverbe, Paris, 1992, p.20. My translation.

135. art and the state
Yoyo Maeght, *The Maeght Family, A Passion for
Modern Art*, Abrams, New York, p.154.

136. time-frames
My text.

137. concentrated awareness
Cartier-Bresson, *Interviews and Conversations*, pp.63, 64.

139. passing years
From Georges Braque's *Notebook, 1917-1947*, published
by Maeght Éditeur, 1947, p.46.

141. art, music, dance
Yoyo Maeght, The Maeght Family, pp.8, 186-193.
My notes.

142. understanding painting
Yoyo Maeght, *The Maeght Family*, p.196.

144. beyond the proscenium arch
My account of the origins and the production of
my first opera, *The Kingdom*, directed by
Rufus Collins in Amsterdam in 1984.

145. My brief evocation of interwoven daylight.

146. morning

147. evening